Word f

W

David Hawgood

Pitman

PITMAN PUBLISHING LIMITED
128 Long Acre, London WC2E 9AN

Associated Companies
Pitman Publishing Pty Ltd, Melbourne
Pitman Publishing New Zealand Ltd, Wellington
Copp Clark Pitman, Toronto

© David Hawgood 1985

MicroPro, WordStar, and MailMerge are registered trademarks of MicroPro International Corporation. CorrectStar, TelMerge and StarIndex are trademarks of MicroPro International Corporation. IBM PC is a registered trademark of International Business Machines Inc.

First edition 1985

British Library Cataloguing in Publication Data

Hawgood, David
  WordStar 2000.—(Computer handbooks)
  1. WordStar 2000 (Computer program)
  I. Title II. Series
  652'.5'0285425   HF5548.115

ISBN 0 273 02357 8

All rights reserved.

Printed in Great Britain at the Bath Press, Avon

Contents

How to Use this Handbook 1
Introduction to WordStar 2000 3
Quick Reminder 7
Stop! Help! Come back! 18
Operating WordStar 2000 26
Files and Documents 33
Typing 40
Editing 67
Page Format 85
Printing 92
Merging Data with Text—MailMerge 97
Windows 112
Manuals 116
Installation 117
Index 123

How to Use this Handbook

After an introduction describing WordStar 2000, this handbook has two reminder sections. The first reminds you how to start the system and operate it. The other reminds you how to stop things happening, how to recover from accidental deletions and other problems, and how to get help from the system.

The handbook continues with reference sections, describing the facilities for typing, editing and printing documents. The final sections describe the installation procedure, manuals, and training aids which form part of this comprehensive word processing package.

Notation

Throughout this book the caret symbol ˆ followed by another character means 'hold down the Control key and press the key for the next character at the same time'. Thus ˆG means 'hold down Control and press G'. This command means 'Get help', to display help screens.

Often Control key sequences can be replaced by function keys. These are printed in braces, { }. For example the alternative to ˆG for getting help is {F1}, meaning 'press function key 1'. The allocation of function keys can be changed during installation. Those given in this book are the ones used as standard on an IBM Personal Computer:

Numbered function keys F1 to F10, alone or with the shift key.

Keys such as 'Home' and 'PgDn' in the cursor movement block, alone or with Control.

Keys in the row of numbers (1 to 9, 0, −, =), with the Alternate (Alt) key.

The computer often replies to a command by displaying a question on the screen. In this book these are printed with the word 'Question:'. After the word 'Answer:', this book tells you what answers WordStar 2000 will understand, and what their effects will be.

The abbreviation (CR) is used for the Return key, which is marked 'Enter' or with a bent arrow as on a typewriter carriage return. The Return key has to be pressed after most answers typed in to the computer. It is not generally mentioned specifically in this book.

Introduction to WordStar 2000

The first thing to tell you about WordStar 2000 is that it is very different from WordStar. It is not an enhanced version, it is a new and improved product. WordStar has been the most widely used word processing package for years. Its manufacturers, MicroPro, have developed WordStar 2000 based on experience with WordStar, users' comments, and competitive word processing packages. WordStar 2000 provides more facilities than WordStar, and is easier to use.

WordStar 2000 is a complete word processing package, suitable for the occasional user or the full time typist. The standard package includes spelling check and correction, and MailMerge. There are still some optional additions: MailList for easy preparation of name and address files, StarIndex for preparing contents and indexes, and TelMerge for sending and receiving electronic mail.

WordStar 2000 uses the function keys and screen facilities of the computer to make operation easier. The first release of WordStar 2000, in late 1984, was for the IBM PC and closely compatible machines. It makes good use of the operating system facilities available.

Ease of use
Simple commands use initial letters of facilities where possible; e.g. ^RS for Remove Sentence, ^BD for Block Display. Function keys are used for common commands—for example Block Beginning is either ^BB (with the Control key) or just function key 9. A template is provided to show the function keys and their uses.

You can get help on any command. Explanation screens and examples are given, then you can return to the point at which you requested help.

Economy of typing
You can set up abbreviations and expansions as a keyword glossary. Type the abbreviation, press Escape, and the expansion appears.

Many of the installation options of WordStar become format options in WordStar 2000. There can be a number of formats—e.g. memo, letter, report, minutes. A format includes choice of page length, width, line spacing, justification, choice of typeface. It can also contain standard text.

Spelling is not just checked: corrections are suggested. There is an extensive general purpose dictionary. You can also create personal dictionaries. These can contain technical terms, special abbreviations, etc.

Choosing documents or other files is easy. You do not have to type the name. You can just move highlighting around the directory on screen, using the cursor keys, till you reach the right one. You can also type the first few characters of the name—the first one matching it is highlighted and can be used without typing the rest of the name.

Printing
WordStar 2000 provides ways of obtaining advanced facilities of printers. These can include justified proportional spacing, coloured ribbon, stationery from different print trays on sheet feeders.

Getting data from organized files
WordStar 2000 provides flexible mail merge facilities. It can deal with far more than just names and addresses—really it provides 'list management'. It can either print a document per item, or a list of items within a document. Combinations of conditions can be applied to choose which items are printed.

Screen display
What you see is what you get, complete with underlining, and highlighting for bold printing. In addition tags describing other print enhancements can be turned on, or off, so the screen layout is the same as the printed layout. On a colour monitor, WordStar 2000 can be installed with different colours for different types of text.

Headers, footers and footnotes
Headers and footers can be chosen separately for odd and even pages. Footnotes can be added, and are automatically numbered and renumbered.

Margins and tabs
Text automatically changes if tabs or margins are changed. The ruler line can be visible in text where the change is made, and applies until the next ruler line in the text.

Windows and other files
Not only can parts of several documents or files be visible on the screen, blocks of text can easily be moved from one to another. You can look at a data file while setting up MailMerge conditions. From one document you can call up the whole of another document to be printed, and return to the original one, chaining or nesting the printing.

'Undo'—get back what you removed
This is available to recover from mistakes, restoring a word, sentence, line or block just removed. 'Undo' can also be used in a planned way. It provides an easy way of moving or duplicating a word, sentence, line, or paragraph, without having to mark a block.

Maths and sorting
WordStar 2000 will calculate down a column or along a line—totalling a column, making extensions along a line. It will also sort complete lines of information.

Optional extras
It combines with optional MailList for easy preparation of name and address files, with StarIndex for preparing tables of contents and indexes, and with TelMerge for electronic mail.

Configuration needed
WordStar 2000 needs a 256K micro. Hard disk is recommended: this makes it possible to have dictionaries for spelling correction available on line all the time.

Security copies of WordStar 2000
WordStar 2000 is copy protected. Three copies of the WordStar 2000 program can be made from an original disk. However a copy can be 'uninstalled' from one place, e.g. a hard disk, and installed again, e.g. on a different hard disk, or on a floppy disk.

Quick Reminder

This section provides a summary of the steps needed to start the system, open a document, type, save, edit, quit and print using WordStar 2000.

What you need—with a hard disk system

It is assumed that WordStar 2000 has been installed, and that a directory has been created to hold your work files.

You may need an operating system disk when turning on the computer. Apart from this, everything you need should be on the hard disk.

Up to the point where you type 'WS2' to load WordStar 2000, the detail of this description is for PCDOS on an IBM Personal Computer, with fixed disk drive C, floppy disk drive A. For other configurations, computers or operating systems there may be small differences.

Turn on the computer. If prompt is A⟩ type C: to give C⟩ prompt. Change directory to the one in which you will be working. For example, if the WordStar 2000 programs are in directory WS2000, and your files are to be in a directory MARY which is a sub-directory of one called SALES, type:

CD \SALES\MARY (CR)

WS2 (CR)

This should give the title screen and opening menu of WordStar 2000.

If WordStar 2000 is installed in the standard recommended way, typing WS2 from any directory on the same hard disk drive as WordStar 2000 should give the opening menu.

Two floppy disk system—what you need

You will need at least an operating system disk, a disk with the WordStar 2000 program installed on it, and a work disk.

If the work disk does not contain the key file, you need a key disk as well.

To run any spelling check and correction, you need a copy of the WordStar 2000 dictionary disk.

To convert a WordStar file to WordStar 2000, or vice versa, you need a copy of the WordStar 2000 conversion disk.

To run StarIndex, MailList or TelMerge you need the advanced features disk.

One drive (e.g. drive A) will at various times contain the operating system disk, WordStar 2000 program disk, spelling disk, conversion disk, or advanced features disk.

The other drive (e.g. drive B) will contain a key disk when starting WordStar 2000, a work disk at other times.

To start: load the operating system, following the instructions for the computer you are using. For example, on an IBM PC put the operating system disk in drive A, turn on the computer. This gives a prompt A⟩.

Put the program disk in A. Put the key disk in B, or put a work disk with a key file in B, and type:

WS2

The title screen should be displayed, followed by the opening menu. If you used a key disk (rather than a work disk with a key file) during loading, remove it from B and put in your work disk.

If the disk in drive B when you typed 'WS2' did not contain a key file, an error message will say that the loading has failed.

Key disks

A key disk is created in phase 1 of the AutoInstall procedure. Work disks containing the hidden key file can be made by making a complete backup of the key disk. In PCDOS the command for this is 'diskcopy'; use the following procedure.

Put a blank unformatted disk in drive B, the operating system disk in drive A.

At the A⟩ prompt, type:

diskcopy A: B: (CR)

Put the key disk in A, press any key to continue.

On completion of this operation, the disk in B is a combined work disk and key disk.

The hidden key file used when starting WordStar 2000 is different from a key glossary file containing abbreviations and expansions.

Drives, directories and paths

Using a system with two floppy disks, your WordStar 2000 program and standard files with it are generally in drive A. You log on to drive A to run WordStar 2000. Your own documents are on a diskette in drive B. To access a file on drive B, you type b: before the filename. The 'Choose a Name' screen of WordStar 2000 makes this easier. If you type b: (CR), the directory of drive B is displayed, but you remain logged on to drive A.

Most operating systems for microcomputers with hard disks allow the disk to be split into directories.

Each directory can contain files and other directories. WordStar 2000 is designed to make good use of this feature. If a computer is used by several different people, each can have a directory containing their own documents. There only has to be one copy of the WordStar 2000 program and the files supplied with it, such as standard formats. These are in their own directory, named WS2000.

If using hard disk, you log on to your own directory. The list of documents, formats, or key files displayed will be the ones in it. To see those in the WordStar 2000 directory, type \WS2000 (CR) from any Choose a Name screen. You will still be logged on to your own directory.

To see files in another drive or directory, you type its path from a Choose a Name screen. See your operating system manual for details of path names.

Typing a new document

From opening menu press E.
Question: Document to edit or create?
Answer: Type the filename you want, e.g. 'minutes'. (If using floppy disks, type the drive letter and a colon before the filename, e.g. 'b:minutes'.
Question: Format to use?
Answer: Names of formats in the logged-on directory are displayed. Those in another directory can be displayed by typing its path. The pre-set ones supplied with WordStar 2000 are:

```
JUSTIFY.FRM  MEMOFORM.FRM  MSCRIPT.FRM  NORMAL.FRM
RAGGED.FRM  UNFORM.FRM      WS2LIST.FRM
```

Others displayed will be those you or others have created before, e.g. MEETINGS.FRM for minutes of meetings.

Use the cursor keys to move the highlighting to the format you need, press Return. A status line and ruler should appear at the top of the screen. Depending on installation options chosen, the list of editing choices may appear between them. If it does not, and you would like to see it, type ^GG {F1F1} and answer A to the question.

Here, and elsewhere in the book, ^ means 'hold down the Control key and press the next key at the same time'. So you press Control and G together, then press G again. G is for Get help. The alternative if you have function keys set up in the standard way for an IBM PC, is to press Function key number 1, twice. In this book, function keys are always shown in braces { }. They include the numbered function keys F1 to F10, keys in the cursor movement block, and number keys with the Alt key.

Although you have just opened a new document, there may be some text displayed already. A format can include standard text to be included in any document with that format. If you are in insert mode, use the arrow keys rather than the Return key to move the cursor down through the standard text. Note that the Tab key inserts another tab, even if you are in overtype mode.

Now type your text. Just keep typing at the end of a line of text. If there is not room for a word on the line it will automatically be moved down to the next line, or hyphenated. Use the Return key at the end of a paragraph, or to give a blank line. Use tabs for any tabular matter or indents.

The ruler line can be changed while typing. The list of tabs and margins commands can be seen by typing ˆT. The new ruler will be saved with the text, at the position where it was changed. There can be a number of different rulers saved with text, each one applying down to the next ruler. If option display is on, rulers are visible in the text.

For correcting mistakes as you type, remember that the arrow keys just move the cursor, 'Delete' or ˆRC erases the character at the cursor, 'Backspace' erases the character before the cursor, 'Insert' or ˆOO changes from overtype mode to insert mode or vice versa. The status line at the top of the screen shows whether you are in overtype or insert mode.

Saving

You do not have to finish typing the document before saving. It is good practice to save regularly. If you have typed enough to be worth saving, or are called away from the screen for a moment, type ˆQC or {3 and Alt}, for Quit and Continue. What you have typed is stored away on disk. After this command, the cursor is replaced at its position when the command was given, so you can just continue typing. It does not matter where the cursor is when you save—everything before and after the cursor is stored.

To Quit and Save, type ^QS {1 and Alt}.
To Quit and Print, type ^QP {4 and Alt}.
If you type a command and want to get out of it, press Escape. This will get you back to the editing screen.

Editing

To view or change an existing document:

At the opening menu, press E.

On hard disk, the names of documents in the current directory will be displayed. Move the highlighting to the one you want, press Return. See description of 'Choose a Name Screen' on page 29 for other methods.

On a system with two floppy disks, type b:(CR) to see the directory of documents on your work disk. Move the highlighting to the one you want, press Return.

Moving the cursor

Use the arrow keys to move the cursor left, right, up or down. {PgDn} moves it down one screen, {PgUp} moves it up one screen.

For end of document, press {Control and PgDn}.

For beginning of document, press {Control and PgUp}.

To move to a specific page, type ˆCP and answer the question with either: the number of the page, + for forward, +n for forward n pages, − or −n for back one or n pages; e.g. −3 moves back 3 pages.

For left-hand end of the line, type ˆCL or {Control and Home}.

For right-hand end of line, type ˆCR or {Control and End}.

For top left of screen, press {Home}.

For bottom left of screen, press {End}.

Making changes

Move the cursor to the place where the change is to be made. Use the 'Insert' key or ˆOO to change to insert mode or overtype mode, type the change.

WordStar 2000 provides a number of 'remove' commands—for character, word, sentence, paragraph, entire line, etc. For all except the single character commands, the 'Undo' command, ˆU or {F2}, will replace the removed text at the current cursor position.

There are two methods of carrying out 'cut and paste' operations. One is to cut out text with a Remove command, move the cursor, and paste in the text by the Undo command. The cursor can be moved and the same text pasted in somewhere else by another Undo. The other way is to mark a block, then copy, move, or remove it.

To mark a block, move the cursor to its beginning, type ^BB or {F9}. Then move the cursor to its end, type ^BE or {F9 and Shift}. A marked block appears highlighted.

To move or copy a block, put the cursor at the position where the block is wanted, type ^BM {F10} or ^BC {F10 and Shift} respectively. Block Remove is ^BR; the 'Undo' command can be used to replace a removed block.

Quitting a document

After making changes which are to be saved, type:

^QS {1 and Alt} for Quit and Save, or;

^QP {4 and Alt} for Quit and Print.

After viewing only, or if changes are not to be saved, type ^QA {2 and Alt} for Quit and Abandon. This leaves the file how it was when it was opened, or how it was left by an intermediate ^QC {3 and Alt} (Quit and Continue).

Quit and Print leads through a series of questions about the printing of that document. Quit and Save or Quit and Abandon lead to the opening menu.

Print

A document can be printed by typing ^QP from editing it, or by pressing P from the opening menu and choosing the filename to print.

You will be asked a series of print decision questions. To accept all default answers, type ^Q. This prints one copy of the complete document with no pauses between pages. Other choices are described in the section of this book on printing.

Note that the page length, line spacing, line width, etc. are decided when selecting a format. To change them, type F from the opening menu, then type the name of the file you want to change (preceded by the drive letter on a floppy disk system).

Making copies of WordStar 2000

WordStar 2000 is copy protected. The installation procedure allows up to three copies to be made onto hard disk or floppy disk. Copies cannot be made by the operating system copy or backup utilities. Copies can be 'uninstalled' from a disk and 're-installed' onto another disk, or another directory.

This particularly affects security and recovery procedures on hard disk systems. Details are given with notes on installation procedures.

Do not delete the program WS2000.EXE. Use the 'uninstall' procedure.

Do not install WordStar 2000 in RAM disk (random access memory simulating a disk).

To move WordStar 2000 from one directory or drive to another, uninstall and re-install.

The manufacturers recommend that WordStar 2000 should be uninstalled before a directory containing it is backed up, and re-installed after backup, or after recovery.

Note that the copying restriction only applies to the program WS2000.EXE. It does not apply to other programs or files in the system.

Stop! Help! Come back!

To stop printing from the printer

On most printers there is a switch or button marked 'on line'. The quickest way to stop is to use this. Change it to the 'off line' position. This gives you time to work out what to do. When you change back to 'on line' WordStar 2000 should continue from where it left off. Even if you decide to start printing again from the beginning, you should change the printer back to 'on line', then quickly interrupt the printing from the computer as described below.

To stop printing from the keyboard

If not editing another document
If you chose not to edit another document while printing, or still have the opening menu displayed, press P.

Question: Printing is interrupted: Continue or Abandon (C/A) C
Answer: Press C or Return to continue, press A to abandon the print run.

Printing may continue until the printer buffer is empty.

If editing another document
Type ˆQP {4 and Alt}.

If you are not on the editing menu, press Escape. Depending what else you were doing, it might be necessary to press Escape several times. The 'Continue or Abandon' question is displayed as described above. After answering, you will be able to continue editing.

To abandon a print run when a question is displayed, asking you to change stationery or type an answer, proceed as follows. Answer the question, then quickly type ˆQP or {4 and Alt} to stop the resumption of printing.

Stop other operations

Pressing Escape stops most operations, and gets you out of most questions. It usually takes you back one stage in the route you have followed from the editing menu. You have to be careful not to overshoot: pressing Escape at the editing menu may start a key glossary expansion.

Lost menu or file

If the list of choices available in the editing menu or a sub-menu does not appear when you expect it, type ^GG or {F1F1}; answer A to have All menus displayed, or S to have sub-menus displayed.

If you know you saved a document but cannot see its name displayed in the directory, it is probably on another drive or directory. From the Choose a Name screen, type the path for other directories you have used. On a hard disk, look in the root directory, and the WS2000 directory. On floppy disks, look on the other drive.

If a format, key file or dictionary is lost, there is another possibility. WordStar 2000 only displays formats with extension .FRM, key files with .KEY, dictionaries with .DCT. But WordStar 2000 allows you to build such files with a different extension, or none. The solution is to go to the opening menu, choose M for move/rename, move highlighting to the filename with the wrong extension, rename it with the correct extension.

Help!

The help screens of WordStar 2000 are very useful. They provide information about the menu, screen, or command from which they are requested. They give instructions, examples and useful hints. It is always worth having a look at the help screens, particularly for facilities you do not use often.

From the opening menu, press G.

From an editing menu, Choose a Name screen, or Decisions screen, type ^G (G stands for Get help) or press {F1}.

If G is followed by a letter on the menu, the help screen gives information relevant to that menu choice. For example, GK from the opening menu displays a screen about Key glossaries.

To get back from help screens to what you were doing, press Escape.

Come back!

If you remove some text and wish you hadn't, use the Undo command. Type ^U or {F2}.

The last text removed will be inserted at the current cursor position. This applies to all Remove commands except Remove Character, Delete, and Backspace. If you have performed any other operations since the removal, or moved the cursor, the text is inserted at the new cursor position rather than its previous location.

If you are editing a file and would prefer to keep the old version not the new one, type ^QA (Quit and Abandon changes) or {2 and Alt).

If you have saved a file, and think you might prefer the previous version, you can use the backup copy. At the opening menu, press C for Copy. Move the highlighting to the file with the same name as the one you have just saved, but with extension '.BAK', for example FILENAME.BAK

At the question 'File to copy to?' it is best to choose a different name, e.g. SAFECOPY.BJH. A file with the extension .BAK cannot be viewed, edited, or printed, but the new copy can be.

21

Out of space

If you get an 'out of space' message while editing, and want to keep your changes, first try to Quit and Save, ^QS. WordStar 2000 creates a temporary disk copy of a document while editing is in progress. The space required on the disk is more during editing than when saving. Once you are back to the opening menu, you can make any necessary backup copies and remove unwanted files.

If you have several windows (see page 112) open, Quit and Abandon the files you are not editing.

On a floppy disk system, remember to put the drive letter in front of the filename, e.g. b:filename. If you forget, the system will try to create a file on the WordStar 2000 program disk, which has little space on it.

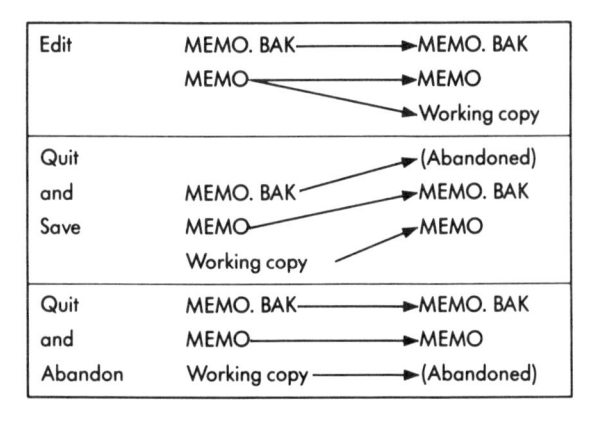

Edit	MEMO. BAK ─────────► MEMO. BAK
	MEMO ─────────► MEMO
	↘ Working copy
Quit	► (Abandoned)
and	MEMO. BAK ─────► MEMO. BAK
Save	MEMO ─────► MEMO
	Working copy ↗
Quit	MEMO. BAK ─────────► MEMO. BAK
and	MEMO ─────────► MEMO
Abandon	Working copy ─────► (Abandoned)

Figure 1. Versions of a document file.

Backup files

Figure 1 shows a file, its backup, and the temporary working copy of it.

Unexpected results from printer

If the print enhancements produce unexpected results, and you cannot see an obvious mistake in your document, print the file PRINT.SPL. This will print examples of all the enhancements and features available on the installed printer. If this output is wrong, the installation procedure for the printer which is connected to the system has not been carried out correctly. If the output from PRINT.SPL is right, look again for mistakes in your own document.

If MailMerge produces unexpected results, see notes on testing in the section of this book describing the merging of organized files, page 111. Because WordStar 2000 can obey complicated conditions, it has to be very particular in its evaluation of expressions. If your condition looks right but produces unexpected results, try putting brackets in the condition, or writing several simple expressions to produce the same result.

Keeping your data safe

Save early and save often
Quit and Continue saves the file, then returns the cursor to its position so you can continue typing. Use it every ten minutes, or just after a complicated piece of typing, or just before an extensive piece of editing.

Copy your files to another disk
You can use C from the WordStar 2000 opening menu to copy a file to another disk, typically from fixed disk to a diskette which can be taken away for safe keeping. The operating system provides good facilities for making backup copies—see the manual for your computer. This gives ways of copying files which have been changed. It is good practice to make a copy of changed files every day.

Probably the easiest way, though not the most economical in disks, is to make a copy of the complete contents of any floppy disk or hard disk directory with changes.

For floppy disks, use a cycle of three, e.g. red, blue, and yellow. At any time there are two in the cupboard and one in use. At the end of the day copy today's work disk to the oldest of the others, e.g. red to blue, blue to yellow, yellow to red on successive days. Today's work disk goes in the cupboard, the copy becomes tomorrow's work disk.

For hard disk, the simplest way is to use a similar cycle, making a complete copy of your directory onto the oldest backup. Security is much easier if document files are kept in directories separate from the one containing the WS2000.EXE program.

Recovery

If a file is corrupted or lost and you have to recover from a security copy, make another copy before starting to use it. Otherwise, if the same fault or mistake occurs again, you may find you have corrupted your security copy as well as the working copy.

If recovering from WordStar 2000 automatic backup copies, the .BAK file has to be copied to another file before it can be used.

Remember that the WordStar 2000 program WS2000.EXE is protected, and cannot be copied by operating system utilities. WordStar 2000 should be uninstalled before the directory containing WS2000.EXE is backed up, or restored, or deleted, or reformatted.

Operating WordStar 2000

This section describes the method of operating in general. It describes the way to use screens which are displayed by a number of different commands.

Starting WordStar 2000

Turn on the computer and load the operating system.

Two floppy disk system
On a two floppy disk system, put your copy of the WordStar 2000 program disk in one drive, log on to that drive (usually drive A). Put a key disk in the other drive (usually B). Type WS2 (CR). The WordStar 2000 title page should appear, followed soon by the opening menu. The error message displayed if the disk in drive B is not a key disk is not very helpful—for example, 'load error 13'.

Hard disk system
On a hard disk system, log on to the directory containing your work files. The procedure depends on the operating system and configuration in use. The following example is for PCDOS loaded from floppy disk (drive A); the work files are on hard disk, drive C, in a directory JOE which is a sub-directory of one called SALES.

At initial system prompt A⟩, type C: (CR). Computer responds with the prompt C⟩.

Type CD \SALES\ JOE (CR), meaning 'change directory to the one with path \SALES\JOE'.

Type WS2 (CR). The WordStar 2000 title page should appear, then the opening menu.

If WordStar 2000 is installed on hard disk in the recommended way, typing WS2 from any directory loads it. If your files do not appear in the list displayed when you press E from the opening menu, you may be in the wrong directory. Press Escape, type D at opening menu to change directory, type the path for your directory.

Opening menu

There are two opening menu screens. Press the spacebar to move from one to the other.

The following are on both:

Edit/create	Print	Get help
Remove	Copy	Quit

On the first only:

Directory/drive	Key glossary
Move/rename	Typewriter mode
Spelling check	Format design

On the second only:

Access TelMerge	L MailList
WS/WS2000 file conversion	Indexing

Press the key for the initial letter of the facility required. Upper or lower case can be used. For example key 's' or 'S' for Spelling check.

In most cases another menu, or Choose a Name screen, or Decisions screen, is displayed.

Q for Quit from the opening menu gives the operating system prompt A⟩ or C⟩, unless a WordStar 2000 operation is still in progress.

Note that TelMerge, MailList and Indexing are optional extra software packages.

Commands and menus

Many commands are listed in sub-menus, but can be keyed in full, or by function key, from editing.

For example ^P gives the print enhancement sub-menu. With this sub-menu displayed, keying B gives boldface printing.

Alternatively, key ^PB or press function key {F4}.

Some menus can be obtained either fron the opening menu or from the editing menu. For example, to edit key glossary entries from the key glossary menu, type K from the opening menu or ^K when editing.

Choose a Name screen

This screen is used very widely within WordStar 2000. It appears whenever there is a choice from a number of possibilities, other than the pre-set menus. There are several convenient quick methods of choosing one from a number of options. If choosing from files, note that those displayed at first are in the current directory. By typing the name of another drive or directory and pressing Return, you get the same convenient ways of choosing from its set of files.

The screen displays a status line, showing disk drive and directory; the screen name; instructions; a question; a line for the answer; a default answer (initially highlighted if present); and a list of names available for choice (directory of documents, list of fonts, etc.).

There are two active areas on this screen, the answer line and the highlighting. A name can be chosen by typing it in the answer line, or by moving the highlighting to it. When you press Return, anything which has been typed or moved into the answer line is taken as the choice. If the answer line is blank, whatever is highlighted is taken as the choice. Initially a default choice is highlighted. In most cases this is the last file or name used. The highlighting can be moved around the display using the arrow keys.

If your choice is in another drive or directory, there are two ways of obtaining it. One is to type the path and filename, e.g. b:mymemo. Another is to type the path and Return, e.g. b:(CR). The appropriate directory is displayed and you can move the highlighting to the name you want.

As you type into the answer line, the highlighting moves to the first name starting with the characters typed. If for example the directory is:

MEETING   MEMOJOAN   MEMOLEN   MEMOSTAN

Type 'memo'. The highlighting moves to MEMOJOAN. Add s giving 'memos' and it moves to MEMOSTAN.

If the correct name is highlighted and you have typed some characters into the answer line, type ^T. The highlighted name moves into the answer line. Press Return to accept it.

Operations available in Choose a Name screen:

Anywhere·
^G	Get help.
Escape	Go back to what you were doing.
Return	Accept answer line, or highlighted name if answer line is empty.

Editing the answer line:
Backspace	Remove character to left of cursor.
^R	Remove answer, leave answer line blank.
^T	Move highlighted name to answer line.

In directory or name display:
← or ^S	Move highlighting left one name.
→ or ^F	Move highlighting right one name.
↑ or ^E	Move highlighting up one row.
↓ or ^X	Move highlighting down one row.
^W	Scroll up one line.
^Z	Scroll down one line.
^V	View or hide list of names.

Drive, directory and file names can be typed in upper or lower case letters.

If a directory is chosen, you are temporarily logged on to that directory.

For key glossaries, spelling dictionaries and other files the name chosen can be a new one. For fonts, ribbon colours and paper trays it must be an existing one.

After choosing a name, further questions may appear. For example, when removing a file, the question is 'Are you sure?'

Decisions screen

This screen is used when you are asked to make a series of decisions. An example is the set of decisions needed when printing is started.

The screen displays a status line showing drive and directory; the name of the screen; instructions; and a list of questions, with default answers.

If typing an answer, use upper or lower case, or numbers. Yes or No require only their first letters, Y or N.

Controls available are:

^Q	Quit answering: accept default answers for those that have not been changed.
Delete	Remove character at cursor.
Backspace	Remove character before cursor.
^← or ^A	Cursor left one word.
← or ^S	Cursor left one character.
→ or ^D	Cursor right one character.
^→ or ^F	Cursor right one word.
↑ or ^E	Cursor up one line.
↓ or ^X	Cursor down one line.
^R	Remove answer from answer line.
^T	Restore default answer in answer line.
Return	Move to next question.
^V	View one question or all questions.

Function keys

In this book the function keys given are the standard ones for an IBM PC. Other computers may have different arrangements of function keys. A template is provided with the package, showing the initial allocation of function keys.

The allocation of function keys is also shown on two help screens. To see them, press G from the opening menu or ^G from the editing menu; press the space-bar to look through the help screens.

It is possible to change the meaning of function keys, using Phase 2 of the AutoInstall procedure. (see page 121).

Files and Documents

The operating system facilities most likely to be used with WordStar 2000 are available from the opening menu. Used from there, they act on only one file at a time. Facilities available are: Copy; Remove; Move/rename; Directory/drive (to change logged-on directory or drive).

Hard disks can contain large numbers of files. Some are programs, some are data files supplied as part of software packages, some are data files and documents started by different users. To make it easier to find the right file and to control access, operating systems split drives into directories. These are arranged as a tree structure. Any directory can contain both files and other directories.

Figure 2 shows an example. The root directory of disk drive C contains some files. It also contains directories called STORES, SALES, and WS2000. This latter contains WordStar 2000 programs, dictionaries, and formats. WS2000 also contains a directory called TUTORS, with training files. STORES has directories called JOE and SUSAN. SALES has directories called JOE and MARY.

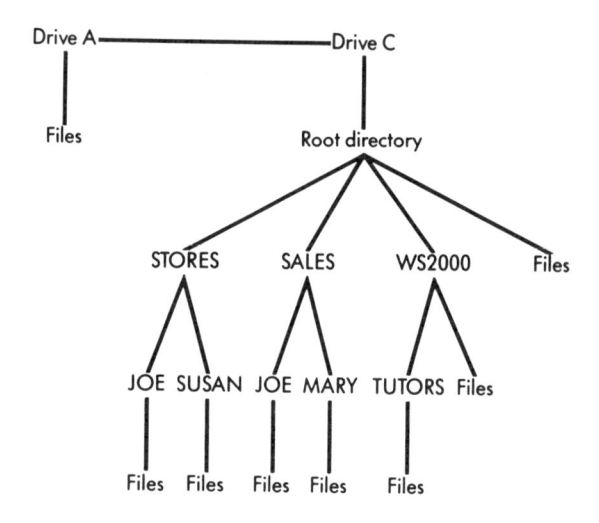

```
Drive A ──────────────── Drive C
   │                        │
 Files                 Root directory
                            │
        ┌────────┬──────────┼──────────┐
      STORES   SALES      WS2000      Files
       / \     / \         / \
     JOE SUSAN JOE MARY  TUTORS Files
      │   │    │   │      │
    Files Files Files Files Files
```

Figure 2. Directory structure.

At any time a user is logged on to one directory. Subject to access restrictions, it is possible to use files in other directories. The series of drive, directory, and sub-directory names needed to reach a particular file is called the path.

WordStar 2000 is organized to take advantage of the available directory structure. On hard disk, for almost all purposes, you log on initially to your own directory, and use document files within it. Access to the WordStar 2000 program is automatic. See the *WordStar 2000 Installation Guide* for details of this.

If using twin floppy disks, your programs and documents will be on different drives. You will have to give the drive letter when you select a filename. For example, type b:minutes to get a file called minutes on drive B. An alternative is to type b: (CR) and move the highlighting to 'minutes'.

Copy file. C from opening menu

Displays Choose a Name screen (see page 29).

Question: File to copy from?
Answer: Move highlighting to filename, or type filename (with path if not in current directory).
Question: File to copy to?
Answer: Type filename, and path if necessary.

The new contents of 'file to copy to' are now the same as those of 'file to copy from', which are not altered. Any previous contents of 'file to copy to' are removed.
  Examples:

* In directory SALES\JOE, to copy the format file MEMOFORM.FRM from WS2000, calling the copy JOESMEMO.FRM:

  Copy from? Type WS2000, press Return. Move highlighting to MEMOFORM.FRM, press Return. Copy to? JOESMEMO.FRM

* In directory SALES\JOE, to copy the file GOODNEWS onto a floppy disk in drive A, giving the file the name KEEPNEWS:

Copy from? Move highlighting to GOODNEWS, press Return.
Copy to? A:KEEPNEWS

* With a twin floppy disk system, to copy the backup file CHAPTER2.BAK on the work disk in drive B, and make another copy on drive B, with the name CHAP2OLD, to open for viewing or editing:

Copy from? B:CHAPTER2.BAK
Copy to? B:CHAP2OLD

Remove file. R from opening menu

Displays Choose a Name screen (see page 29).

Question: File to remove?
Answer: Move highlighting to selected filename, or type it (with path if not in current directory).
Question: Are you sure? (Y/N)
Answer: Press Y to remove, N or Return to keep it.

Press Escape at either question if no file is to be removed.

Move or rename a file. M from opening menu

Displays Choose a Name screen (see page 29).

Question: File to move or rename?
Answer: Move highlighting or type name (with path if necessary), press Return.
Question: New location or new name?
Answer: type new filename, or path for new location.

The file is now available with its new name or location, and is no longer available with its old name or location.

Example: you need the space on hard disk occupied by a file, but want to keep it on floppy disk in case it is needed. The file is PROPOSAL. It is to be moved to a diskette in drive A.

* File to move? move highlighting to PROPOSAL, press Return.
  New location? type A: (Return).

Change Directory or drive. D from opening menu

Displays Choose a Name screen (see page 29).

Question: Change directory or drive to?
Answer: For drive, type its letter and a colon, e.g. B: (CR). For directory, type its path, then Return. If you want a sub-directory of the one you are in, move highlighting to its name, press Return.

This change remains in force until another change is requested.

Note that a temporary change of directory can be made within the Choose a Name screen, and applies only while the particular command is executed. For example type C (for Copy) from the opening menu, then WS2000 (and Return) to see the files in the WordStar 2000 directory. You can select one of them by moving the highlighting to it and pressing Return. This procedure can be used to copy a format to your own directory, so that you can modify it to suit yourself.

Quit WordStar 2000. Q from opening menu

This returns you to the operating system prompt in the drive and directory to which you last changed. If you come out of WordStar 2000 without meaning to, type WS2 to come back in. Default answers will have changed back to their initial settings.

Space remaining and file sizes

To see how much disk space is left on a drive, quit WordStar 2000 and use operating system commands. For example in PCDOS, DIR shows space remaining on the drive, and displays a list of files with the space taken by each one. DIR MYMEMO shows space remaining, and the size of the file MYMEMO. DIR JOE*.* gives a list of all files in the current directory with names starting JOE, with space taken by each and space remaining. See your operating system manual for instructions for this type of command.

Filenames

Your operating system will give rules for filenames. A typical rule is:

A filename must start with a letter, then can have letters or numbers, maximum eight characters including the first letter. Optionally these can be followed by a full stop and a file extension of up to three characters.

Examples of valid filenames are A, A1, A.DOC, ABCDEFGH.IJK, SALESMAY.RPT.

Certain file extensions are used as standard by WordStar 2000.

.BAK	Backup
.FRM	Format
.DCT	Dictionary
.KEY	Key glossary
.DTA	Data files for MailMerge
.SPL	Sample files for training

Other file extensions are used as standard by operating systems. For details, see the manual for your computer. Examples are .BAT .SYS .EXE .CMD.

Avoid having two document files with the same name but different extensions. There will be confusion about their backup files. It is best to use extensions only as an indication of the type of document, for example .RPT for all reports.

Typing

WordStar 2000 gives easy access to many helpful facilities while typing and can be used at different levels. It is very simple for the occasional user but includes very sophisticated features which can save even more time for users who are not skilled typists. It is well worth becoming familiar with the range of facilities available.

Key glossary
This allows you to type an abbreviation, and have it expanded automatically to its full form. It is worth using for words, phrases and sequences of commands used even a few times in a document. It is particularly convenient for entries which need a specified format, such as references to books and articles. It is also worth using for systematic editing of a document.

Spelling correction
If you are not sure how to spell a word, make a guess. By entering one command, ^OSW for Option Spellcheck Word, you can get a succession of suggested correct spellings.

Arithmetic
As you type you can get WordStar 2000 to calculate. For example, it will multiply out 23 items @ 7.57 each, doing arithmetic along the line and recognizing the @ sign for multiplication. It will also add a column of figures. All this is done quickly as you type.

System data
The date, time, page number, line and filename can be obtained and automatically printed.

Merging organized data files
You can easily take data from an organized file. This has many more uses than sending form letters. It is often worthwhile for a list or table, especially if the information is likely to be used again in a different way. You can select a few items from a larger list by combinations of conditions. This is all done from within WordStar 2000, while typing a document.

Windows
The windows facility allows you to have parts of two or three different documents visible on the screen at the same time. You can look at an old document, and move parts of it into the current document. You can look at a data file while typing the commands to merge it with your document. You can look at a spreadsheet, move part of it into your document, and add bold printing or underlining where you want them.

Function keys
Use of function keys makes typing very much easier. The package as supplied includes a template showing their specific uses.

Formats with standard text

When you open a document for the first time, you choose one from a library of pre-set formats. These have page length, line spacing, margins, etc. They can also have standard text included in them. This could be a standard letter, a memo heading, or a standard agenda for a meeting. This feature saves a great deal of time in dealing with the everyday correspondence of an office or club secretary.

Opening a document

If you are opening a new document, decide in advance what format to use. There are seven pre-set ones supplied with WordStar 2000. You can design others to suit your own document—see page 85.

Whether you are starting a new document, editing an old one, or opening one to view its contents, press E (for Edit) from the opening menu.

The Choose a Name screen is displayed, with the list of files in the logged-on directory or drive. If the list is not displayed type ^V to see it.

Question: Document to edit or create?
Answer: For a new document, type its filename. You will then be asked to select a format. For an existing document, move the highlighting to the name, press Return.

The quick reminder section on page 7 gives more information on opening a document.

Typing—what you see

If the menu display is set to 'sub-menus only' or 'none', there will be a status line and a ruler line at the top of the screen, followed by your text. To get the editing menu displayed, type ^GGA. In the WordStar 2000 documentation, the screen display with text and cursor displayed ready for typing is referred to as the editing menu, whether or not the list of choices is displayed.

The editing menu complete with list of choices is shown in Figure 3.

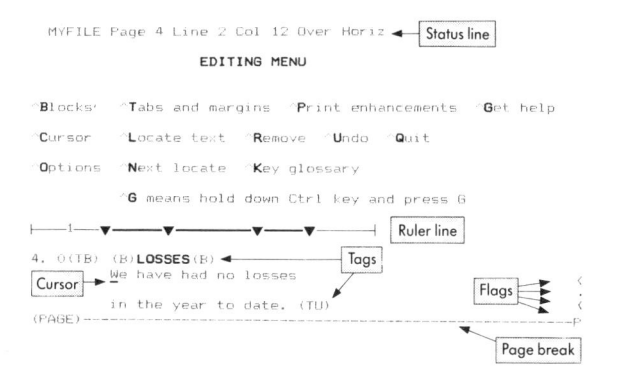

```
MYFILE Page 4 Line 2 Col 12 Over Horiz  ◄── Status line
                    EDITING MENU

^Blocks   ^Tabs and margins   ^Print enhancements   ^Get help
^Cursor   ^Locate text   ^Remove   ^Undo   ^Quit
^Options   ^Next locate   ^Key glossary
          ^G means hold down Ctrl key and press G
├────1───▼───────▼───────▼───▼───┤  Ruler line
4. O(TB)  (B)LOSSES(B) ◄── Tags
Cursor ──► We have had no losses                    Flags
          in the year to date. (TU)
(PAGE)-------------------------------------------P
                                    Page break
```

Figure 3. The screen when typing.

43

The status line shows the command in use, or WAIT if WordStar 2000 is busy. If several windows are open, the status line applies to the one containing the cursor.

'Page' is the screen page number, which always starts from 1 at the beginning of the document. The printed page number can be set to start from any desired number. 'Page' in the status line may also show that the cursor is in the text of a header, footer, comment, footnote, or unformatted file (UNFORM) which has no page breaks.

'Line' is within the page.

'Column' is measured in tenths of an inch, to correspond to the position on the printed page. It is not a count of character positions. (This is described later with tabs and margins.) Note that if the selected typeface has more than ten characters per inch, there will sometimes be two characters in one column.

'Over' or 'Insert'. If 'Over' is displayed, a keyed character overtypes the character at the cursor position. If 'Insert' is displayed, the character at the cursor is moved to the right. The paragraph automatically reforms to the set margins and indents as text is inserted. To change from 'Over' to 'Insert' or vice versa, type ^OO or press {Insert}.

'Horiz' or 'Vert'. A block can be defined in either horizontal mode or vertical mode. If vertical, it is a column with top left at the start of block marker, bottom right at the end of block marker. If horizontal, the block runs from the start marker to the end of that line, then along the whole of each line until the end of block marker is reached. To change from one mode to the other, type ^BV (Block Vertical).

The display of menus is optional. To change, type ^GG or {F1 F1} then: A for all menus, S for sub-menus only, N for no menus.

Ruler line
The ruler line which applies at the position of the cursor is always visible at the top of the window showing the document. It can be wider than the screen. If option display is on, other ruler lines may also be visible. See the description of tabs and margins on page 52.

Cursor
The cursor is in the window of the file being edited. It may disappear temporarily while actions proceed. To move it to another window, type ^CW (Cursor to Window), or {F3 and Shift}.

Flag Column
This is at the far right of the screen (see table for explanation).

Flag	Meaning
.	Line does not continue to right of screen.
+	Line does continues to right of screen.
⟨	End of paragraph. 'Return' on that line.
P	Page break (with hyphens across screen).
C	This line is text or tag for unprinted comment.
F	This line is text or tag for a footer.
H	This line is text or tag for a header.
N	This line is text or tag for a footnote.
–	This and the next line print on the same line. (See ^PN in print enhancements.)

Note that comments, footnotes, etc. are not displayed if option display is off. ^OD, {F1 and Shift}, turns it on or off as a toggle.

Appearance of text

If option display is on, command tags are shown on the screen, tabs are shown, the text of comments and footnotes is shown.

If block display is on, the text of a block is highlighted (or coloured). To turn it off type ^BD. Note that you cannot copy, move, remove, sort, write or perform arithmetic on a block if block display is off.

The appearance of text is changed depending on the monitor and graphics card in use, and the installation options chosen.

On monochrome monitors, highlighting, reverse video, and underlining are used. Boldface, subscript, superscript, strikeout, and emphasized characters are highlighted. So is the part of a ruler line in use if indents are in operation.

On a colour monitor colours can be chosen separately for various backgrounds and types of text. If you come across an unfamiliar colour in text, turning on option display will usually show the tag which caused it.

Block and cursor markers

⟨B⟩ is the beginning of block marker. ⟨E⟩ is the end of block marker. If either of these is visible the block is not yet fully marked, and block operations will not work. A marked block is highlighted.

⟨0⟩ to ⟨9⟩ are cursor markers, set by ^CM. The cursor is moved to marker 9 by ^C9, and correspondingly for other digits.

Justification, hyphenation, and word-wrap

The appearance on the screen is the same whether justification is on or off. The initial setting at the start of the document is set as part of the format. Note that it is not an installation option. If the format has justification on, typing ^OJ, with option display on, will produce a tag [JUSTIFY OFF]. The next ^OJ will cause [JUSTIFY ON], and so on.

Automatic hyphenation is another format option. If it is off, any word which will not fit on a line will be moved to the start of the next line. If automatic hyphenation is on, a word which will not fit will be split. Hyphenation rules are built-in to WordStar 2000. Positions of hyphens in individual words can be controlled by the ^O− command.

Print enhancements

These are commands which control the appearance of the text when printed. Most are in the sub-menu obtained by typing ^P, some are in the sub-menu obtained by typing ^O.

For the following commands, put the cursor where the enhancement is to start then key the command. Move the cursor on to the place where the enhancement is to stop, and key the same command again.

Effect	Type	Function key	Tag displayed
Boldface	^PB	F4	[B]
Underline	^PU	F4 and Shift	[U]
Emphasis	^PE		[E]
Strikeout	^PS		[S]
Subscript	^P−		[−]
Superscript	^P+		[+]
Justify	^OJ		[JUSTIFY ON] or [JUSTIFY OFF]

Depending on the particular printer in use, emphasis and boldface may be achieved by printing the character twice or three times in the same place, or with a small displacement, or with other changes.

Strikeout prints hyphens across the printed characters, ~~like this.~~

^OJ for change of justification should be used only at the beginning of a paragraph.

Spaces between words can be underlined or not, as a format choice.

Centering ^OC

Type ^OC or {F2 and Shift} with the cursor anywhere on the line to be centred. If option display is off, the text will be displayed centred. If option display is on, the tag [CENTER] appears at the beginning of the line, with the text pushed to the right of centre.

To move centred text back to the left margin, put the cursor anywhere in the centred line and type ^OC again.

Printer options: line spacing, font, colour, paper tray

The options available depend on the printer installed. When the command is issued, WordStar 2000 displays a list of the options available on the installed printer, and asks you to choose one. This is done by moving the highlighting to the required option with the cursor keys, then pressing Return. The initial font and line spacing (line height) are chosen as part of the format, the initial colour of printing and print tray from which to take stationery are defaults—usually black print on plain paper.

On some printers, the 'colour' command is used for an alternative set of fonts, e.g. italics.

Print Height (line spacing) ^PH

Position the cursor at the start of the first line of changed spacing, type ^PH.

The Choose a Name screen is displayed with a list of available spacings. For example:

Question: Line height (spacing)?
        6.00 LPI (highlighted)
        3.00 LPI   4.00 LPI   6.00 LPI

In the format, 6.00 LPI has been chosen, giving single spacing. This will be the highlighted default the first time the ^PH command is used. If double spacing is required, move the highlighting to the required spacing (here 3.00 LPI), press Return. If option display is on, a tag will appear with the selected line height, e.g. [3.00 LPI].

Font, typeface ^PF

To change from one font to another, type ^PF.

Question: Font to use?
Answer: Move the highlighting to the required font, and press Return.

The names of typefaces are abbreviated. For example [NON PS 12] is a monospaced, 12 characters per inch typeface.

On daisy wheel and similar printers, a change of font requires a pause in printing. Type ^PP as well as ^PF. On buffered printers, the pause only takes effect at the end of a paragraph.

On some printers an alternative set of fonts can be obtained by plugging in a different module. Again, ^PP to pause printing is needed.

If colour is not available, the command ^PC 'Print Colour' may be used to select other options on a printer. On some printers, a set of italic typefaces is obtained from ^PC.

Print the file PRINT.SPL to see a sample printout of all the features available on your printer. Also look at the README file; this lists printers and says which of their facilities are supported.

Print Colour ^PC

Question: Ribbon color to use?
Answer: Names of colours available are displayed, e.g. BLACK, RED.
Move the highlighting to the one you want and press Return.

Paper Tray ^PT

Question: Paper tray to use?
Answer: Names of types of stationery available are displayed, e.g. PLAIN PAPER, LETTERHEAD. Move the highlighting to the one you want and press Return.

The ^PT command should be issued at the start of text, or at the end of a page of text, above the page break indicator.

The Ruler

The initial ruler line for the document is set as part of the re-usable format. This is chosen when the document is first opened. The current ruler is displayed on the screen, at the top of the window displaying the document.

```
|——————▼——————▼2——————▼——3——#——4—|
```

	represents the margins. The format includes the offset of the left-hand margin on odd and even pages.
▼	represents a normal tab stop; the screen display for this is a bright triangle.
#	is a decimal tab stop.
Digits 1 to 9	are measurements in inches across the printed page.
—	(hyphen) represents other columns. There is one for every tenth of an inch on the printed page.

Note in particular that tab positions are in tenths of an inch, not in character count. This allows columns of data to be aligned even if the typeface is changed. It is essential for proportional spacing, where different characters have different widths.

When any tab and margin command is issued except one which only changes indents, a new ruler is created. If option display is on, this is visible above the line of text in which it is created.

At top of window: |―――▼―――▼2―――▼―3――#―|
In text: L―――!―――!―――!―――#―R

Tabs and margins in a ruler line in text are shown as follows.

	Top of window	In text
Left margin	|	L
Right margin	|	R
Regular tab stop	▼	!
Decimal tab stop	#	#
Inch markers	Digits	―
Other columns	―	―
Indent	Highlight	Tags TB TI TO TU

Margins

Tabs and margins Left
^TL {F7}   Set left margin.

Question: Left margin in what column?
Answer: Any number from 1 to 70. It must be at least 9 columns to the left of the right margin. If no number is entered, the margin is set at the current cursor position. Result (with option display on): The new ruler line is displayed above the line containing the cursor. Text below, to the next ruler line, is reformed to comply with the new ruler.

Tabs and Margins Right
^TR {F7 and Shift} Set right margin.

Question: Right margin in what column?
Answer: Any number from 10 to 240. It must be at least 9 columns to the right of the left margin.
Result: As for Tabs and margins Left.

Indentation

There are four commands to change indentation.

^TB Tabs and margins Both margins in.
   Both margins move in one tab stop.
^TI {F5} Tabs and margins In left.
   Left margin moves in one tab stop.
^TO {F5 and Shift} Tabs and margins Out left. Left margin moves outward one tab stop.
^TU Tabs and margins Undo all indentation. All indentation is cancelled.

If option display is on, the relevant tag [TB], [TI], [TO], or [TU] appears in the text.

For all four, if the cursor is at the start of the line the command takes effect immediately. If the cursor is not at the start of the line, the command takes effect on the next line.

Several indentation commands can be issued together on one line. ^TI ^TI moves the left margin in two tab stops. ^TU ^TI cancels all indentation, then sets the left margin at the first tab stop.

Following text automatically reforms if any of these commands is issued.

If any indentation command is active, the part of the ruler line between the current left and right margins is highlighted.

Set and unset tabs

Note that there are two ways of selecting the column at which to set or unset a tab. The first is to move the cursor to the column, then issue the command. The tab is set or unset in the column containing the cursor. The other method is to issue the command, then type the column number at which to make the change. Remember that column numbers are in tenths of an inch, not in numbers of characters. The result is that a tab appears or disappears in the ruler at the top of the window. Text from the line containing the cursor to the next ruler is reformed. If option display is on, a ruler line appears above the line containing the cursor.

Tabs and margins Set tabs
^TS {F8} Set a regular tab stop.

Question: Set tab in what column?
Answer: Return alone sets a tab at the cursor position, a column number sets a tab at the specified column.

Tabs and margins Decimal tab stop
^TD   Set a decimal tab, for aligning numbers.

Question: Decimal tab in what column?
Answer: Return alone sets a decimal tab at the cursor position, a column number sets one at the specified column.

Note: leave room for at least two characters between the decimal tab and the right margin.

Tabs and margins Clear tab stop
^TC   {F8 and Shift}   To clear one or all tab stops.

Question: Clear tab in what column (A for ALL)?
Answer: Type A to clear all tabs, Return alone to clear tab at the cursor position, column number to clear one at the specified column.

Note on tabs and rulers

The maximum number of regular and decimal tab stops in a ruler is 30.

A ruler can be removed by ^RE or ^RW. After removing the ruler, it can be put back in the same place or a different place by the Undo command, ^U or {F2}. Alternatively, a ruler can be marked as a block with ^BB and ^BE, then copied with ^BC.

If there are some rulers you use regularly it is worth setting up a file with copies of them all, e.g. with filename RULERS. When you want one: Open a window with ^OW or {F3}, answer RULERS. Move cursor to window with ^CW or {F3 and Shift}. Move cursor to the ruler line you want, type ^RE then ^U, or {F6 and Shift } then {F2}. Close the RULERS file by ^QA, or {2 and Alt}. Move cursor where you want the ruler, type ^U or {F2}.

Using tabs

The Tab key always inserts a tab, whether you are in overtype mode or insert mode.

To move from tab to tab without disturbing text: Type ^L for Locate text. Press the Tab key, and Return twice. This accepts all default choices in locating. The cursor moves to the first tab character after the cursor. Type ^N to locate Next tab character. Keep typing ^N to move from tab to tab.

Decimal tabs

If you want a column of numbers to be aligned, use a decimal tab.

The rule is that a number, up to its decimal point, is aligned to the left of the decimal tab. The decimal point, or first non-numeric character, is placed at the tab. Subsequent characters follow on to the right of the tab. A space is not a numeric character.

The character used for alignment can be changed to comma during installation of WordStar 2000. The thousands marker is changed from comma to full stop at the same time.

Examples, with alignment on full stop as decimal:

```
─────#─────
     .01
    2
   21.01
 1234
 1,234                 Thousands marker.
     1 234             Space is not numeric.
         About 2.0     Letter is not numeric
```

Key glossary

While typing you can define an abbreviation and its expansion. After that, every time you type the abbreviation followed by the Escape key, the expansion appears in the text.

A number of key glossary files can exist. Each can contain up to twenty entries. The name of the one in use is displayed in the status line of the key glossary menu. Type ^K to see it.

Key files can also be created or changed by choosing K from the opening menu.

Key glossary menu
^K   A list of commands available is displayed, and you can Get help on these facilities.

Key—Use another key file
^KU   Names of available key files are displayed on the Choose a Name screen.

Question: Key file to use?
Answer: Move highlighting to select an existing one, or type a new name to create one. Press Return.

Names of key files must include the extension .KEY (for example DAVID.KEY). WordStar 2000 does not warn you if you omit the extension when you choose a name, but it does create the file. You can subsequently use the Move/rename facility from the opening menu to add the extension .KEY.

Key Define
^KD
Question: Short form to define.
Answer: Type one to fifteen characters, letters or numbers only. Press Return.
Question: Long form? (Press ^Q to end)
Answer: If an existing short form was typed, the corresponding long form is displayed and can be edited. Otherwise, type the long form you want, then ^Q.

A long form can be up to 560 characters, the maximum for all long forms in a file is 2000 characters. There can be up to 20 short and long forms in a file.

To include commands type caret (^) not the control key.

When all short forms have been defined, press Escape.

Question: Should these changes be saved?
Answer: Y to save, N or Return not to save.

After N or Return the changes can be used until you use the ˆKU command or quit Wordstar 2000.
After Y to save:

Question: Key file to use?
Answer: To create a new key file, type its name, with extension .KEY (preceded by b: on two floppy disk system). To change current key file, which has name highlighted, press Return.
Question: That file already exists—Replace? (Y/N)
Answer: Y to save, N or Return not to save (as after 'Should these changes be saved?').

Editing a long form: For cursor movement, use arrow keys or ˆA, ˆD, ˆE, ˆF, ˆS, ˆX as in editing (see page 67). Then:

Delete	Removes character at cursor.
Backspace	Removes character to left of cursor.
Return	Ends paragraph, or adds a blank line.
ˆR	Removes a line of text.
ˆQ	Ends a long form.

Key Remove
ˆKR
Question: Short form to remove?
(Names of available short forms are displayed).
Answer: Move highlighting to select short form, press Return to remove, press Escape to make no further changes.

After pressing Escape:

Question: Should these changes be saved? (Y/N) N
Answer: Y to save new version, N or Return to restore previous version.
Question: Key file to use?
Answer: proceed as in Key Define, ˆKD.

To use a short form

First make sure the cursor follows a space, a Return, or a stand-alone tag in a document being typed or edited.
   Type the short form, then press Escape. The result is just as if the long form, including any control sequences, had been typed.

Headers and footers

The header and footer appear on the page on which defined, and on subsequent ones. Odd and even pages can have different headers and footers.

Options menu
ˆO   The header and footer are among the miscellaneous facilities on the option menu.

Option Header
ˆOH   Before typing this command, put the cursor at the top of the first page to include the header.

Question: Both odd and even pages?
         Odd pages only?
         Even pages only?
Answer: Press B, O, or E (without Return).

Two tags appear, with the cursor on the line between
them, for example:

[EVEN HEADER]   H
(cursor)   H
[EVEN HEADER]   H

Type the text of the header, one or more lines, then
move the cursor outside the tags. To remove a header,
remove all the text between the tags.

The system inserts one blank line between the header
and the text. If line height (line spacing) is changed by
using ^PH within a header, this applies to all
subsequent headers but not to text. If there is no ^PH in
a header, the current setting for the text is used. The
same applies if a ruler is defined in a header.

The page number can be included in a header by
using the system variable &%page&. If doing this, use
the format facilities to remove the automatic page
number from the footer.

Option Footer
^OF   Footers work in the same way as headers. Put
the cursor at the top of a page, before or after a
header, type ^OF. Answer B, O, or E and type the text.

Page length, header, and footer

The header and footer, and the blank line inserted automatically between each and the text, are allowed for in calculating page length. For example if paper length is 66, top and bottom margins 5 each, header 1 (plus one blank left automatically), footer 2 (and 1 blank) the text is 66 − (5 + 5 + 2 + 3) = 51 lines. The automatic page number available as part of the format counts as a one line footer.

Footnotes

Wordstar 2000 automatically numbers footnotes consecutively in a document, and adjusts the numbers if a footnote is added or removed. When printed, footnotes appear at the end of the document, with a reference number as a superscript in the text where defined. The footnote command is on the options menu. Option display should be on when defining footnotes.

Option footNote
^ON   Move the cursor to the place the superscript reference is required, type ^ON. Two tags appear, with the cursor between them.

```
... as quoted by Hoskins [FOOTNOTE]           N
(cursor)                                      N
[FOOTNOTE]. However ...
```

This will be printed:

... as quoted by Hoskins[2]. However ...

The last ruler in the text of the document applies to footnotes, unless a ruler is defined within a footnote. If you want a blank line between footnotes, include it in the text between the footnote tags. The manufacturers of WordStar 2000 recommend insertion of a page break at the end of a document, so that footnotes appear on a new page.

Quit

Quit editing menu
^Q   Displays menu.

Quit and Abandon changes
^QA   {2 and Alt}   If you have edited the document in any way:

Question: This document has been changed. Abandon anyway? (Y/N)
Answer: Y to abandon changes, N to return to editing menu.

If no changes have been made, ^QA is the right command to use. This occurs for example if the document has been opened for inspection, or to copy a block out of it. It is only the changes which are abandoned, not the complete document.

If two windows are open on one document, ^QA has to be used on one of them before the other can be saved. If both contain changes you want to keep use ^BW (Block Write as a file), or ^BC (Block Copy) into the other window, to save changes.

Quit and Continue
^QC {Alt and 3}   The current document and changes to it are saved, then you can continue editing. The cursor will not have moved. Use this to safeguard changes at regular intervals, or if you have to leave the screen for a moment.

Quit and Save Changes
^QS {1 and Alt}   The current document is saved. The opening menu is displayed.

Quit and Print
^QP {4 and Alt}   This has the same effect as ^QS to save changes, followed by selecting P for Print from the opening menu. The Decisions screen is displayed, with the first question: Begin printing on what page?

^QP cannot be used if more than one window is open.

If another document is already being printed, ^QP interrupts it with the question 'Printing is interrupted: Continue or Abandon? (C/A) C'

After answering, you are returned to editing your current document. It will not have been saved, and will not be printed as a result of this command.

Typewriter mode

In this mode WordStar 2000 prints text either character by character, or line by line, as you type it. There are no tabs, margins, page offset, or print enhancements. In line (buffered) mode, the line of text can be corrected before printing.

From opening menu, press T for Typewriter mode. The printer should first be turned on, switched online, with paper loaded. The following commands are available:

^B	Turns line buffer on or off.
^Q or Escape	Quit typewriter mode, back to opening menu. First press Return, to print your last line.
Return	In buffered mode, prints the line. In unbuffered mode, with a buffered printer, prints the line. In unbuffered mode, with an unbuffered printer, does a carriage return.

To find out whether your printer is buffered, press ^B to change to unbuffered mode. Press the space-bar a few times. If the print head moves, the printer is not buffered.

Editing the buffered line

^A	Cursor one word left.
^S or ←	Cursor one character left.
^D or →	Cursor one character right.
^F	Cursor one word right.
Delete	Remove character at cursor.
Backspace	Remove character before cursor.
^R	Remove all text from line.
Return	Print the line.

The maximum line length is the width of the screen, 80 characters. If you continue typing at the end of the line, characters are lost. You have to press Return at the end of the line. There is no word-wrap.

Editing

Cursor movement in text

Cursor left one word	^A {^ and ← }
Cursor left	^S { ← }
Cursor right	^D { → }
Cursor right one word	^F {^ and → }
Cursor up	^E { ↑ }
Cursor down	^X { ↓ }
Scroll screen up one line	^W
Scroll screen down one line	^Z
Cursor menu	^C

A menu of available cursor movement commands is displayed.

Cursor to Page number   ^CP
Question: Go to which screen page number?
   (Press + for next page or − for last)
Examples of answers (any number can be used):

- 7   Goes to screen page 7.
- +7   Moves forward 7 pages.
- −7   Moves back 7 pages.
- +   Moves to next page.
- −   Moves to previous page.

In all cases, the cursor goes to the first character of the selected page. These numbers are screen pages—they are not affected by use of ^OA to assign page number.

Cursor to Left margin	^L {^ and Home}
Cursor to Right margin	^R {^ and End}
Cursor Home (upper left of window)	^CH {Home}
Cursor to end of window (lower left of window)	^CX {End}

Cursor Down one screen	^CD {PgDn}
Cursor Up one screen	^CU {PgUp}

The text moves up or down to show the next section.

Cursor to Beginning	^CB {^ and PgUp}
Cursor to End	^CE {^ and PgDn}

These move the cursor to the beginning or end of document respectively.

Cursor to beginning of block	^CA
Cursor to end of block	^CZ
Cursor to Old block's position	^CO

This moves the cursor back to the last position from which a block was moved.

Cursor to marker number 0 (similar for markers 1 to 9)	^C0 ^C1 to ^C9

Cursor to another Window	^CW {F3 and Shift}
Cursor to footNote	^CN

Question: Go to which footnote number
  (press + for next footnote or − for last)?
Answer: Similar to ^CP, Cursor to Page. 3 goes to footnote 3, +3 goes on three footnotes, −3 goes back 3 footnotes, etc.

Cursor To character   ^CT
Question: Character to go to?
Answer: Press a character key (including punctuation symbols, Tab key)
Result: Cursor will move to next occurrence of that character.

Cursor—set a Marker   ^CM
Question: Set which marker (0 – 9)?
Answer: Type one digit, for example 5.
Result: ⟨5⟩ appears on the display at the cursor position, with the cursor to the right of it. It is shown whether or not option display is on. The marker is set, whether or not the same marker was present elsewhere in the document. If the instruction is repeated with the cursor immediately following the place marker, it is removed. Place markers are not printed.

Removing text

Remove: to see menu   ^R

Remove Character at cursor   ^RC {Delete}
Remove character before cursor   {Backspace}
The effect of the above two commands cannot be reversed by 'Undo'. The effect of all other remove commands can be reversed. 'Undo' is ^U or {F2}. These two commands do not remove a stand-alone tag such as [B]. Use ^RW or ^RE instead.

Remove Word ^RW {F6}
Removes word containing cursor, or all but one of a series of successive spaces.

Remove Entire line ^RE {F6 and Shift}

Remove Left side of line ^RL
Removes characters on line to left of cursor.

Remove Right side of line ^RR
Removes character at cursor, and all others to right of it on the line.

Remove Sentence ^RS
Removes from the character following the preceding full stop up to and including the next full stop.

Remove To a character ^RT
Question: Remove from cursor to what character?
Answer: Type a character.
Result: Text is removed from the character at the cursor to the one preceding the next occurrence of the character typed, or paragraph end or page end if sooner.

Remove Paragraph ^RP

Remove Block ^RB
This does nothing if block display has been turned off with ^BD (but is not affected by option display, ^OD).

Undo ^U {F2}

The last text removed is inserted at the current cursor position. If the cursor has not been moved since the remove command, the text is re-instated in its original position. The cursor can be moved and 'Undo' can be used any number of times to insert the removed text anywhere in the document, or in another window. The removed text is available until you use another remove command, or quit editing all files and return to the opening menu. Although a block can be moved by 'remove and undo', this is not recommended for a vertical block. Use ^BM instead.

Block operations

Blocks menu ^B

Block Begin
^BB {F9}   This marks the beginning of a block, to include the character at the current cursor position. A marker ⟨B⟩ appears, unless there is already a block end marker set later in the text, in which case the new marked block is highlighted. Block display is turned on automatically when a block is marked. If 'vertical' is on, the end of a block must be below and to the right of the beginning.

Block End
^BE {F9 and Shift}   This marks the end of a block to end with the character before the cursor. The new marked block appears highlighted if there is a preceding block beginning marker, otherwise a block end marker ⟨E⟩ appears. (See also Block Begin.)

Block Display
^BD   This turns on and off the highlighting of a marked block. It is different from option display, ^OD, which turns on and off the display of tags, rulers, comments, footnotes, etc.

The block markers remain in place when block display is off. When a block is marked, block display is turned on automatically.

If block display is off, the following do not operate: Block remove, copy, move, write, sort, perform arithmetic.

Block Vertical
^BV   This allows moving, sorting, and arithmetic operations on columns. When keyed, the indicator in the status line is changed from 'Horiz' to 'Vert' or vice versa.

When vertical is on, the end of a block must be to the right of the beginning of the block. The maximum column width is 240 characters.

Block Move
^BM   {F10}   This command inserts the marked block before the cursor. This applies whether you are in overtype mode or insert mode. Place markers are not moved. The marked text disappears from its original position.

If vertical is on, the marked block is inserted with its top left-hand corner at the cursor position.

A block can be moved from one window to another. Tags and rulers are always moved with the block.

Block Copy
^BC {F10 and shift}   The marked block is inserted at the cursor position, just as for block move, but in this case the original text remains. The newly inserted block is now marked as a block. Place markers are not copied.

Block Remove
^BR The marked block, and the markers, are removed (unless block display is off).

You can use the 'Undo' command ^U to replace a block removed by ^BR. However be careful if 'vertical' is on. Any paragraph of more than one line will have reformed when the block was removed.

Block Insert file
^BI The Choose a Name screen appears.
Question: Document to insert?
Answer: Move highlighting to required filename, press Return. The default is the last file used in a Block Insert or Block Write operation.

The complete document is inserted into the current document, at the current cursor position. The format of the inserted file is not copied. There does not have to be a marked block in the inserted document.

If vertical is on, the document is inserted as a column at the cursor position, if there is room within the margins. Otherwise, the text following the cursor is moved down below the inserted document.

Block Write to file
^BW   The Choose a Name screen is displayed.
Question: File to write to?
Answer: Type filename, press Return. The marked block is copied to form the whole of the named file. The format section is not copied, and any format previously in the destination file is destroyed. Rulers and tags are copied.

Block Sort
^BS   Before you give this command, vertical must be on. The command moves whole lines into order, sorting on the first 20 characters of the column.

Question: Sort orders
           Ascending Descending
Answer: Press A or D

Sorting now proceeds in order of ASCII values of characters:

Space !"#$%&'( )*+,−./0123456789:;⟨=⟩?@
Upper case letters, symbols, lower case letters, symbols.

See the ASCII chart for your system for the sort order of symbols, punctuation, and currency signs. The order is changed according to the national character set in use.

If several lines have the same value in the sort column, their order is unpredictable.

The manufacturers advise that lines to be sorted should be single spaced.

Block Arithmetic

^BA Arithmetic proceeds along lines if horizontal is on, down colums if vertical is on. The answer is placed at the current cursor position.

Note that there is an installation option to choose either point or comma as the decimal marker, and also to choose comma or point as the thousands marker. In the description that follows, it is assumed that point is the decimal marker, comma is the thousands marker.

A number can include one decimal point. A number can be up to 13 digits: the decimal point is counted as a digit. A number can contain commas: these are ignored.

An answer that would have over 13 digits is shown as a line of * symbols.

Addition: + sign or no symbol	2 3	= 5
	2 + 3	= 5
Subtraction: − sign or ⟨ ⟩round number	5⟨3⟩	= 2
	5 − 3	= 2
Multiplication: * or @	3 * 2	= 6
	3 @ 2	= 6
Division: /	3 / 2	= 1.5
Exponentiation: ^	3 ^ 2	= 9
Evaluate first: brackets	2*(3+3)	= 12
	2*3+3	= 9

Order of evaluation: expressions in parentheses
  exponentiation
  multiplication or division
  addition or subtraction

Spaces between numbers are only required if adding horizontally without + signs; apart from this they are ignored. A line break or Return acts as a space.

If the cursor is at a decimal tab stop, the answer will be aligned to the tab stop. In vertical arithmetic, the numbers do not have to be aligned.

Characters evaluated are:

0123456789 + − *@/^,.( )⟨ ⟩

All other characters are ignored.

Spelling correction

For spelling checking and correction, the dictionary files have to be available. This brings differences between hard disk and floppy disk systems. On the latter, disk changes are required.

The following table shows how disks are loaded in a two floppy disk system at various phases of operation. It assumes the two drives are A and B.

A	B	Phase
Boot disk		Turning on computer
WS prog. disk	Key disk	Typing WS2 to get Wordstar 2000
WS prog. disk	Work disk	Typing and editing
Dictionary	Work disk	Spelling correction
WS prog. disk	Work disk	Typing and editing

The first time in a session that you give a spelling correction command, you will be asked:
Name of personal dictionary to use?
If the personal dictionary is on your work disk, type b:filename.dct.

If your personal dictionary is on the dictionary disk it can contain about 1000 words. On the work disk, several personal dictionaries of up to 1500 words can be held.

When requested, replace the WordStar 2000 program disk with the Dictionary Disk. The spelling correction commands and other necessary WordStar 2000 commands are available. On completion of spelling correction, you will be prompted: Replace the Dictionary Disk with the WordStar 2000 Program Disk. Press Escape.

On a hard disk system, there will be the prompt: Name of personal dictionary to use? You will be able to select it by moving the highlighting. None of the disk changing prompts will appear.

Option Bypass spell check
^OB   This command allows a portion of text to be protected from spelling check and correction. It can be used for text or tables containing mainly proper names, specialized expressions, abbreviations, etc.

On first typing ^OB, a tag appears:

[BYPASS SPELLING CHECK ON]

At the next ^OB, the displayed tag is:

[BYPASS SPELLING CHECK OFF]

If the cursor is in the middle of a paragraph, ^OB inserts a Return character as well.

^OSW (spellcheck word) works within a bypassed block, ^OSP (spellcheck paragraph) does not.

Option Spelling menu
^OS   This menu is also obtained by typing S from the options menu, or S from the opening menu. In the latter case, it is preceded by a question: Document to spell check?

Option Spelling Select personal dictionary
^OSS   See notes above if using floppy disks.

Question: Personal dictionary to use?
Answer: To use an existing dictionary, transfer its name to the answer line and press Return.

   To create a new dictionary, type its name and press Return. Include the extension .DCT in the name.

   With floppy disks, to use a dictionary on your work disk, type b: followed by filename.dct.

   The spelling checker CorrectStar creates a personal dictionary called PERSONAL.DCT the first time it is used. All dictionaries must have the extension .DCT.

Option Spellcheck Word
^OSW   {5 and Alt}   This checks the word the cursor is on, or the next word if on a space. A repeat checks the next word. This command operates anywhere, even within a block bypassed by use of ^OB.

Option Spellcheck Paragraph
^OSP   {6 and Alt}   This checks the complete paragraph containing the cursor.

Option Spellcheck Rest of document
^OSR   {7 and Alt}   This checks from the cursor to the end of the document.

While ^OSW, ^OSP, or ^OSR operate, the spelling correction menu appears. When CorrectStar finds a word which is not in the dictionaries, it displays any suspect word, and the suggestion for a replacement. The following are the answers you can make:

(CR) Correct as suggested.
C   Correct all occurrences. This takes effect as CorrectStar goes through the document.
I   Ignore suggestion. Use this for words you know to be correct, but don't want to add to your personal dictionary. The word will be ignored if found again later in the document.
N   Next suggestion. CorrectStar makes another suggestion or 'Suggestion not found' when it has no more alternatives.
P   Previous suggestion. This goes back through suggestions.
A   Add to personal dictionary. The word as spelt is now included in the personal dictionary currently in use.
T   Type correction. Type in another spelling for the word. CorrectStar will check it against the dictionaries. If not found you can Ignore or Add, or go through suggestions for alternatives to the new spelling.
Escape Discontinue spelling check, go back to editing menu.

After spelling correction, use ^QC, ^QS or ^QP to save the changes that have been made.

Locate and replace ^L

^L searches through text for any combination of characters, tabs, paragraph endings, and control tags. The search can be forward or backward, by characters or complete words only, independent or dependent of case. 'Wild card' characters can be used. Every nth occurrence of the characters can be found, for example every third.

When replacing text, the maximum number of replacements can be selected. Replacement can proceed automatically, or the user can confirm each one as it is found. Automatic replacements can be displayed briefly. Text can be replaced exactly as typed, or it can match the case of the characters located.

^N, Next locate, repeats the last location or replacement command you issued.

Location if no options are chosen
WordStar 2000 searches forward for the first occurrence of the characters typed, independent of case, as a complete or partial word. For example 'cat' will find 'cat' or 'Cat' or 'Cathedral'.

Replacement if no options are chosen
WordStar 2000 searches forward to the end of the document. At every occurrence of the characters to be located, it stops and asks you whether to make the replacement. The replacement matches the case of the characters located. For example, it matches a capital letter at the beginning of a sentence.

If replacing 'organis' by 'organiz':

'organisation' will become 'organization',
'Organisation' will become 'Organization',
'organising' will become 'organizing'.

Rules for locate and replace

If location is to include headers, footers, footnotes or tags, turn on option display with ˆOD.

If locating a word in which you have used ˆO−, option hyphen, turn off option display.

From the editing menu, press ˆL for Locate.

Question: Text to locate?
Answer: Type up to 40 characters, press Return.
Question: Locate/Replace (L/R)
Answer: L or just Return for Locate, R for Replace.

If you chose R:

Question: Replacement text?
Answer: Type up to 40 characters, press Return.
Question: Options?
Answer: If locating, type any combination of B (Backwards), C (Case), W (Word) and a number, or Return alone for no options.

If replacing, type any combination of B, C, W, D (Don't ask), P (Preserve case), S (Show) and a number, or Return alone for no options. (S can only be used with D.) Meanings of options are explained below.

If replacing without option D for Don't ask:

Question: Replace? (Y/N)
Answer: Y to replace, N or Return alone not to replace.

This 'Replace (Y/N)' question and answer repeats for the number of times selected as an option, or to the end of the document. Press Escape any time to stop the search.

Options when locating
B or b   searches backwards, from the character before the cursor to the beginning.
W or w   locates complete words only: 'cat' finds 'cat' but not 'catch'.
C or c   matches the exact upper/lower case combination: 'Green' finds 'Green' but not 'green'.
Any number n   finds the nth occurrence: option 2 when locating [U] would find every second underline tag, a convenient way to check that the tags are in pairs.

Options can be combined in any order. Some valid answers are '3W' or 'W3' or '3' or 'BWC3'—or just press Return for no options.

If an option is not chosen, the opposite is assumed. Thus if you do not include 'W' in the options, the characters will be located in the middle of a longer word.

The cursor is placed at the beginning of the located string of characters. If searching for a tag, it is placed before the tag, and must be moved before continuing the search with ^N, Next locate.

Options when replacing
B or b for Backwards, C or c for Case, W or w for Word, all as in locating. Any number n, replaces the next n occurrences of the word being located. '3' changes all three roses in 'A rose is a rose is a rose', but no subsequent ones.

P   preserves the case of the replacement text, independent of the case of the located text. Replacing 'manager' by 'President' with option P, either 'manager' or 'Manager' becomes 'President' (so long as you do not choose option C as well).
D   'doesn't ask'. Replacement proceeds automatically without confirmation.
S   'shows replacements'. It can only be used with D, and shows each replacement on the screen for a moment before proceeding automatically to the next one. Press Escape to stop replacement.

Typing the text to locate

Special characters and tags to be found are enclosed in square brackets.

[?] acts as a 'wild card', accepting any character. 'Organi[?]e' finds 'Organise' or 'Organize'.
[#] accepts any digit. A[#] finds A1 or A2 but not A.
[R] (or [r]) finds a Return character, the end of a paragraph or a blank line.
[T] (or [t]) or the Tab key finds a tab character.

You can put several occurrences of one special character in a set of square brackets, [???] or [##], but you cannot combine them. To find 1st or 2nd or 3rd, use [#][??], not [#??].

Tags are typed with their brackets, e.g. [B] for turning bold printing on or off.

If you want to find a special character which is in brackets in the text put a backslash first. For example \[?] finds [?]. \\ finds a single backslash.

Typing the replacement text

[R] or [r] produces a Return, paragraph end, or blank line. [T] or [t] produces a tab character.

You can type a complete tag including brackets, for example replacing [U] by [B]. The tag must not include any variables. A backslash shows that the actual characters typed are required, not a tag. \[U] produces a U in brackets, not an underline tag.

You cannot use a composite tag as a replacement; for 'bold and underline' use [B][U], not [B,U].

Page Format

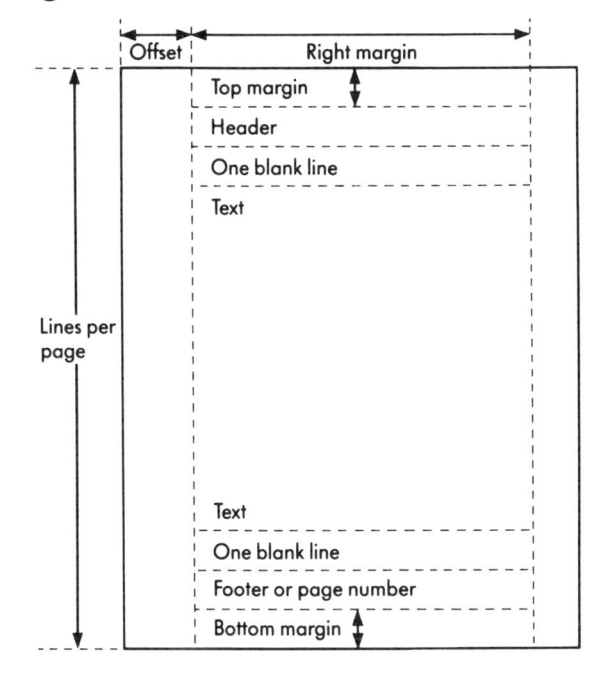

Figure 4. Page format.

In WordStar 2000 different pre-set formats can be prepared for different types of document. Standard text can be added to the format. When another document is first opened, page layout and standard text are included by selection from the directory of formats.

The format of an individual document can be subsequently changed.

Decisions are taken for the format which in other word processors are taken at installation time, at printing time, or by including commands in the text, such as a dot commands in WordStar.

Lines and columns

Distances across the page are measured in columns each one tenth of an inch wide, whatever character pitch is in use. With proportional spacing or compressed print, there may be several characters per column. A right margin of 50 gives a line length of 5 inches. With 10 characters per inch this gives 50 characters per line, but with 12 characters per inch it gives 60 characters per line. If tabs are set every 5 columns they are half an inch apart. With 12 characters per inch, they would be every 6 characters.

One of the first choices is the line height (spacing) in lines per inch. All distances down the page are measured in terms of these lines. With 3 lines per inch on 11" long paper, choose 33 as lines per page. For a 1" top margin, choose 3.

Procedure for setting a format

There are three stages. Preparing a format. Adding text. Choosing a format for a new document.

Preparing a format

From the opening menu press F for Format. The Choose a Name screen is displayed, with a directory of available formats. A format filename has the extension .FRM, for example MEMO.FRM.

Question: Format or formatted document name?
Answer: Type the filename for your new format, with the extension .FRM. Press Return. The Choose a Name screen is displayed, with names of available fonts.
Question: Font to use?
Answer: Move highlighting to font you require press Return.

The names of fonts displayed are those for the printer which has been installed in AutoInstall phase 2. The font names give both the typeface design and the spacing in characters per inch, e.g. NON PS 10 and NON PS 12. The names depend on the particular printer installed, and may not correspond to the names given in the printer manual. The font can be changed in the text of a document by the command ^PF.

On some printers, alternative fonts are available by use of plug-in ROM modules. The command ^PC, Print Colour, may be used to access these.

Question: Line height (spacing)?
The Choose a Name screen is displayed, with a list of available spacings in lines per inch, e.g. if triple, double and single spacing are available on the printer the list would be:

2.00 LPI   3.00 LPI   6.00LPI

Answer: Move highlighting to the spacing required, press Return.

Temporary changes to spacing can be made within text by using the command ^PH, Print Height. This can also be used within a header, footer or footnote.

The Decisions screen is displayed, with a series of questions. See page 31 for general information about the Decisions screens.

Question	Valid answers (default in brackets)
How many lines in the top margin?	0 to 500 (6)
How many lines in the bottom margin?	0 to 500 (6)
Right margin in what column?	10 to 240 (65)
Note: line length in tenths of an inch.	
Set tab stop at every n columns — enter a number for n:	(5)
Note: minimum is right margin divided by 30.	
Number of lines per page?	3 to 500 (66)
Note: usually paper length times 'line height'	
Even numbered page offset in columns?	0 to 132 (10)
Note: margin in tenths of an inch.	
Odd numbered page offset in columns?	0 to 132 (10)
Note: margin in tenths of an inch.	
Text Justified or Ragged-right?	J for Justified,
Note: can be altered in text.	R for Ragged (J)

Automatic hyphenation on? (Y/N)	Y for Yes,
Note: cannot be altered in text.	N for No (Y)
Use form feeds when printing? (Y/N)	Y for Yes,
Note: if in doubt, use N.	N for No (Y)
Underline between underlined words?	Y for Yes,
Note: cannot be altered in text.	N for No (Y)
Display page breaks?	Y for Yes,
Note: affects display only, not print.	N for No (Y)
Page numbers: Centred, Left, Right	C,L,R,A, or N (C)
Alternating or None (C,L,R,A,N)	

Note: these are in footer. A puts page number on left of even pages, right of odd pages. For page number in header choose N, then use ^OH in text to define header.

After answering all questions, or if you press Escape as answer to any question, the Quit Format menu appears:

Press S to save your new format.
Or press C or Esc to continue making changes.
Or press A to abandon the changes you've made.

Notes on answers to questions
Automatic hyphenation: if on, a word that will not fit at the end of a line is split according to rules built-in to WordStar 2000—splitting into complete syllables, splitting at double consonants, etc. The position of a hyphen in an individual word can be chosen by the command ^O−, Option hyphen, in text.

Page breaks: there are ways of finding the page breaks if their display is off. ^CP, Cursor to Page, positions the cursor at the beginning of a page. The status line shows the page number and line number.

Underline between words: the result from answer Yes is like this, from answer No it is like this.

Form feeds: WordStar 2000 can either issue a form feed signal to move to the top of the next page, or issue an appropriate number of line feed signals. Use of form feeds is quicker. It depends on the printer having the facility, and being set to the correct length of page.

Adding text to a format

To change or add standard text in a format, open the format for editing by pressing E from the opening menu, choosing the format filename, then typing or editing text.

Changing a format

The format options can be changed in either a format file or a document file. Press F from the opening menu, choose the format or type the document name, answer the format questions.

Changing the format file does not alter documents which have already been opened using that format.

Duplicating a format

The format is a file like any other, and can be copied. Press C from the opening menu, choose the format as 'File to copy from?', type a new name with the extension .FRM as 'File to copy to?'. For example copy MEMOFORM.FRM to JOESMEMO.FRM. You can then change the format of JOESMEMO.FRM without affecting other people who use the system and want the standard format MEMOFORM.FRM.

Unformatted files

Choosing the format UNFORM.FRM creates files with no format section. These are used for lists of data, source code of programs, and similar files which are not text.

The whole of an unformatted file is regarded as one page. The ruler line cannot be changed. It has a left margin of 1, tab stops every 8 columns, and no right margin. The manufacturers recommend that lines should not contain more than 1000 characters. Justification is always off.

Print enhancement commands, ^P, and Tab and Margin commands, ^T, cannot be used.

The only Option commands that can be used are ^OO overtype, ^OR repeat, ^OS spelling check, and ^OW open window.

Key files, personal dictionary files, and files created by ^BW, Block Write, are unformatted.

Formatting an unformatted file

Press E from the opening menu, type a new filename, choose the format you want.

Type ^BI, Block Insert a file. Choose the name of the unformatted file. It will be copied into your new formatted file, and can be saved by ^QS.

Printing

Printing of a document can be started from the opening menu by choosing P, or from editing a document by typing ^QP, Quit and Print. In either case, you can choose to continue with other work such as editing another document while printing.

There are also options to choose which pages to print, how many copies, whether to pause between pages, and whether to obey formatting tags.

'Printing' to disk
You can choose to send the document in printed format to a disk file instead of the printer. This is useful for checking that MailMerge and other commands are working as expected. It is also useful for creating a file without control codes. This is easier to transfer to other computers. However, note that print formatting commands can produce odd results. For example, bold printing may triple each letter: BBBooollldddd.

Procedure to start printing

Make sure the printer is connected, turned on, switched online, with paper lined up.

If editing the document which is to be printed, use Quit and Print, ^QP or {4 and Alt}. This saves the edited file, then skips to the Decisions screen at the first question, 'Begin printing on what page?'

From opening menu, press P. The Choose a Name Screen is displayed, with a list of files in the logged-on directory.

Question: Document to print?
Answer: To choose the last document edited, which is the default, just press Return. For another document, move highlighting to its name. If not in the current directory, type its path and name, e.g. 'b:minutes'.

Procedure from here is the same whether printing has been started from the opening menu or editing menu. The Decisions screen is displayed with the first of a series of questions. To have all the questions and their default answers displayed, type ^V.

To accept the default answer of one question, press Return. To accept all default answers, type ^Q. The default answers print one copy of the complete document, obeying formatting commands, without pausing between pages.

First question: Begin printing on what page? 1
Answer: Type the number of any screen page. Note that screen page numbers are not affected by use of ^OA to assign different printed page numbers.
Question: Stop printing after what page?
(L for Last)L
Answer: Any screen page number equal to or greater than the answer to the previous question; or L to print to the end of the document.
Question: Print how many copies? 1
Answer: A number between 1 and 1000.
Question: Pause between pages for paper changes? (Y/N) N
Answer: Y for Yes if you will have to change paper or check alignment between sheets; N for No if using continuous paper or a sheet feeder.
Question: Obey page formatting commands? (Y/N) Y
Answer: Y to act on formatting tags, N to print the actual tags but not obey them. For example using Y, [PAGE] moves the paper to the top of the next page. Using N, [PAGE] just prints the characters [PAGE].
Question: Print and continue working? (Y/N) N
Answer: Y to allow you to use other facilities of WordStar 2000 while your document is printed, N for printing alone.

The manufacturers recommend use of N if your document is very long, or contains any Print Pause commands, or uses any of the ^OM MailMerge commands.

If you answer Y, you can then use any opening menu command except I for indexing, L for MailList, or T for Typewriter mode. P from the opening menu interrupts printing.

Question: Send document to printer or disk? (P/D) P
Answer: P for Printer, D for Disk.

If you answer D, the Choose a Name screen is displayed with the question: Disk file to send document to? If you choose an existing file, its contents will be over-written. See note above (page 92) on use of 'printing to disk'.

After answering all questions, you are asked to make sure the printer is ready and press Return.
Printing should commence.

To stop printing

If you answered 'N' to 'Print and continue working?' the screen will display:

Printing (filename). Press P to stop printing.

If this message or the opening menu is displayed, press P to stop printing. If editing another document, type ^QP or {4 and Alt}; you may have to press Escape first to halt another command.

A buffered printer may not stop immediately. To stop quickly, put the 'on line' switch on the printer to 'off line'.

After stopping by P or ^QP:

Question: Printing is interrupted: Continue or Abandon? (C/A) C
Answer: C to continue printing; make necessary adjustments to the printer first. A will abandon printing of that document, returning to the opening menu (if stopped by P) or the editing menu (if stopped by ^QP).

Printer doesn't print?

Once you answer all the questions and press Return to start printing, WordStar 2000 gives error messages if printing cannot start. Examples are 'Can't connect to printer. Press Escape' or 'Printer out of paper. Press Escape'. You should try to clear the problem by adjusting the printer before you press Escape. When you press Escape, WordStar 2000 makes another attempt to print. It gives the same error message again if it cannot start. It is best to regard any message as meaning 'there is something wrong with the printer'. WordStar 2000 does not provide a convenient way of returning to the opening menu if you cannot fix the printer. Consult the operating manual for your computer for ways of stopping.

Testing the printer

There are several ways of testing the printer from the operating system before WordStar 2000 is loaded. The easiest is to press the 'Print Screen' button on the keyboard (often with Shift). For other alternatives see the *WordStar 2000 Installation Guide*, the README file, or the operating system manual for your computer. Look under 'print' or 'type' or 'device' in its index.

Most printers have a built-in test facility. This will print lines of characters, to show that the printer itself is working.

To test that the printer is correctly installed with WordStar 2000, print the file PRINT.SPL. This has examples of the different print enhancements available.

Merging Data with Text—MailMerge

The facilities described here print information which does not come from the stored text of the document. Printing of names and addresses from a separate organized data file is the best known example. This leads to the group of facilities being called 'MailMerge'. But WordStar 2000 has additional similar facilities. A summary of them follows, with their commands.

* Print the date, time, filename, page, or line; type variable name, e.g. &%date&.
* Ask the operator to supply information at print time; ^OMA.
* Display a message to the operator at print time; ^OMM.
* Type a name or phrase in the document once, use it a number of times in the document; ^OMU.
* Insert the text of a different document, then continue printing the first one; ^OMI.
* Print a list, using data from an organized file; or print the document a number of times, once for each record on an organized file; ^OMS (select), ^OML (load), ^OMR (repeat), and ^OMN (next).
* Conditional printing of a paragraph of text, a line in a list, or a complete document, dependent on the contents of items in the organized file, or other variables; ^OMC (condition), ^OME (end), ^OMO (otherwise).

All of these facilities are available within the standard WordStar 2000 package. The optional extra MailList on the advanced features disk makes it easier to prepare name and address files, but is not needed when preparing text or printing.

Variables

WordStar 2000 can hold a number of variables in an area of store not visible on the screen. Each variable has a name, and some contents. For example a variable might have the name 'Size' and contents 'Large' or contents '2000' or contents 'Very large indeed!'. The contents of variables are strings of characters—letters, digits, or symbols.

Variables can be loaded into WordStar 2000 from a separate organized data file, or from the text of a WordStar 2000 document. They can be keyed by the operator at print time, or obtained from the system at print time.

To use a variable, its name is included in the text with ampersand symbols before and after it, e.g. &Size&. The current contents of the variable are then printed in that place in the text. It is also possible to print a selected number of characters from the contents of the variable, as an abbreviation.

System variables
%date
%page
%line
%time
%filename

These can be used anywhere in a document, and do not require any ^OM commands. Just put '&' symbols before and after the system variables. For example a convenient header for a draft uses three.

[HEADER]
&%filename&   &%date&   &%page&
[HEADER]

This prints the name of the file, the date, and the page number, at the head of every page.

Names of other variables
1. Name must start with a letter.
2. Upper case, lower case or mixed case names are equivalent.
3. Name can have 1 to 31 characters, and can contain letters, numbers, and hyphens only.
4. AND, OR, NOT must not be used as variable names.

Abbreviation: after the variable name put the number of the first character to print, then the number of the last character to print, without spaces.

For example &code(5,7)& gives the fifth, sixth and seventh characters of the current value of the variable 'code'. &code(5,5)& gives the fifth character of 'code'.

System variables always exist. %date and %time are obtained from the operating system. %filename, %page and %line are obtained from within WordStar 2000.

Variables obtained by ^OMA, ^OMU, or ^OML (ask, use, or load) exist from the point at which created until the end of that document, or until over-written.

^OMA—From the operator at print time.
^OMU—In text file of a document being printed.
^OML—In a data file, with select, repeat, load.

Variable names need ampersands, e.g. &variable&, except in:

ASK FOR variable
USE . . . . FOR variable
LOAD DATA variable1,variable2,variable3
REPEAT variable TIMES
CONDITION variable ...

Option MailMerge Use
^OMU   Value and variables are typed in at different places in a document.

Question: Field name for data value?
Answer: Type variable name (without & symbols).
Question: Value to use?
Answer: Type value to be printed.

This must precede the variable name in the document.

Option MailMerge Ask for data
^OMA   Asks operator for contents of variable during printing.

Question: Variable name to ask for?
Answer: Type the name of the variable, without & symbols round it.
Question: Question to display when asking?
Answer: Type question to be asked (use 1 to 54 characters), or Return, which gives the default question 'variable name?'
Question: Maximum characters in response?
Answer: Type a number between 1 and 40, then Return. The default is 10 characters.

It is not possible to select abbreviations from the contents of the variable within the ^OMA command. For example, 'forename(1,1)' cannot be used within ^OMA to obtain the first initial only.

An ^OMA question between a REPEAT and NEXT is asked once every repeat.

Option MailMerge Message
^OMM   Displays a message to the operator while printing.

Question: Message to be displayed?
            maximum 79 characters
Answer: Type the message you want to display.

Example of result displayed when editing:

[MESSAGE &name& — condition not satisfied]

Result displayed when printing, if variable 'name' currently has contents 'Stanley':

Stanley — condition not satisfied

Organized data files

An organized data file for use in WordStar 2000 must be a collection of similar records. A record might contain a club member's name, address, telephone number, and date of joining; or a student's name and examination marks. For a stock item it could contain the part number, description, dimensions, unit of issue, and price.

In a WordStar 2000 data file every record must contain the same number of variables, but variables can all be of different lengths. Variables are separated by commas. Records are separated by 'Return' characters.

Example of a data file:

23,Red,LW1(CR)
49076,Blue,***(CR)
19,Pink,LW2(CR)

Rules in more detail

Fields are separated by commas, records are separated by Return. A field containing a comma or quotes as part of data needs quotes around it. A quotes mark required as data has another quotes mark immediately following.
Example:

Description	Dimension	Unit of measure
Shelf bracket, White	6" x 9"	Box of 6

has to be stored as:

"Shelf bracket,White","6"" x 9""",Box of 6

Every record must have the same number of fields. If a field is empty put two commas. For example:
Oil,,Gallon.

Preparing data files

MailList is an optional extra for WordStar 2000 which makes it very easy to prepare name and address files. You can also type a file into an unformatted WordStar 2000 document. The format is also easy to prepare from a program in BASIC.

Using organized files

When preparing the text of the document you select the name of the file using ^OMS. You say how many records are to be read, using ^OMR. You load the contents of a record into the variables in WordStar 2000, using ^OML. The document text follows, including variable names with ampersands. There can also be conditions incorporating the variables, to determine whether a particular record is printed or not. To read the next record, give the command ^OMN. This returns to the previous ^OMR command, and goes through the text again with another record.

MailMerge commands

Option MailMerge Select data file
^OMS   {8 and Alt}
Question: Data file to use?
Answer: Type the filename, for example sales.dta. A drive and directory can be added; the total characters typed can be up to 63.
Result while editing: [SELECT DATA FILE sales.dta]
Result when printing: If a load command (^OML) is encountered, the next record is taken from the selected file.

Option MailMerge Repeat procedure
^OMR {0 and Alt}
Question: Repeat how many times?
Answer: Type a number and Return, e.g. 7 Return;
or: Just press Return to repeat until the end of data in the selected file.
Result displayed: [REPEAT 7 TIMES]
or: [REPEAT UNTIL END OF DATA]

Option MailMerge Next Copy
^OMN { – and Alt}   Displays [NEXT COPY] at cursor. If printing a page per record, such as a form letter per name and address, the ^OMN should be after ^OP to produce a new page.

[PAGE]
[NEXT COPY]

Option MailMerge Load data
^OML {9 and Alt}   This must follow a select. Variable names are separated by commas.

Question: Variables to be loaded? (separate with commas)
Answer: Type names of variables, separated by commas without spaces. For example:

forenames,surname,title

Result displayed:

[LOAD DATA forenames,surnames,title]

The answer can contain up to 64 characters. You can use several ^OML commands in sequence to obtain all of a record with a number of variables.

[LOAD DATA forenames,surname,title]
[LOAD DATA address-1,address-2,address-3]

Option MailMerge Condition
^OMC   After relevant ^OML if used.

Question: Condition to be evaluted? (maximum 64 characters)
Answer: Type condition, e.g. Region = "South".

Use: =   equals
     < >   not equal to
     <   less than
     >   greater than
     <=   less than or equal to
     >=   greater than or equal to

Also use logical operators (typed with upper or lower case or mixed):

AND And and
OR Or or
NOT Not not

Variable names in conditions do not need & symbols around them. Constant values need double quote marks around them, e.g. "South", "21".

(region = "South") AND (age < "21")

This selects people who live in the South and are aged less than 21.

106

(region = "South") OR (age < "21")

This selects people who live in the South, of whatever age, and also selects people aged under 21, wherever they live.

(region = "South") NOT (age < "21")

This selects people who live in the South and are not less than 21. It can also be expressed:

(region = "South") AND (age >= "21")

A condition can be 1 to 64 characters long. Parentheses give priority of evaluation; e.g.,

Age < "21" AND (region = "South" OR region = "West")

is different from:

(Age < "21" AND region = "South") OR region = "West"

The first gives people less than 21, in either the South or the West. The second gives everyone in the West, and those less than 21 in the South.

If brackets are not used, rules of precedence determine the result. Brackets may make the condition easier to understand even when they are not strictly required.

Option MailMerge Otherwise
^OMO   This must be after ^OMC.

Result displayed: [OTHERWISE]

Result when printing: Any text or commands between [OTHERWISE] and [END CONDITION] are printed or obeyed if the condition is false, i.e. the condition is not satisfied.

Note that a CONDITION must have an END CONDITION, but OTHERWISE is optional.

Option MailMerge End
^OME   This must be after ^OMC, and ^OMO if used.

Result displayed: [END CONDITION]

There must be a preceding CONDITION, and can be a preceding OTHERWISE.

Labels

For 'several-across' labels, follow detailed instructions given in the *WordStar 2000 Reference Guide.*

Comparison

Comparisons are between strings of characters, whether they are letters, digits, or symbols. The order is space, symbols, digits, symbols, upper case letters, symbols, lower case letters, symbols. See an ASCII code table for your system to see the order of punctuation marks and other symbols. In comparing two strings, the first characters of each are compared, then the second characters, etc. The strings following come in the order shown:

```
09
21
39
9               (9 is after 3)
Lion
Tiger
lion            (lower case l is after upper case T)
lion and tiger
lioness         (e is after space)
```

If you want number comparisons to be correct, all numbers must be the same length, with preceding zeros if necessary.

Order of evaluation in comparisons

Parentheses
Variable (can be abbreviated)
Comparison characters
NOT
AND
OR

Spaces do not affect the condition, as long as they are not in the middle of a variable name, or within a comparison character.

Every condition must have a corresponding END CONDITION.

Up to eight pairs of CONDITION and END CONDITION can be nested.

Example:
We are writing to announce our new product.
[CONDITION age < "21"]
We are making a special offer to everyone under 21: you can buy three for the price of two.
[CONDITION region = "South"]
As you live near our distribution depot, we are making the offer even better—delivery is free.
[OTHERWISE]
The delivery charge is shown in the attached brochure.
[END CONDITION]
[END CONDITION]

Result:
Everyone gets a letter about the new product.
Those under 21 get told about the special offer.
Those under 21 in the South get free delivery.
Those under 21 elsewhere are told about the delivery charge.

Techniques for testing

Make a test 'print' to a file instead of to paper. For example, use a filename TESTRUN.

Open that file TESTRUN for editing;
Open a window on the master document;
Open another window on the datafile.

You can now look at the condition, the data, and the result, all on the screen together, to make sure the result is what you expected.
   An alternative approach is to use the MESSAGE facility (^OMM), with a pause in printing to allow time to read the message.

[CONDITION region = "South"]
As you live near our distribution depot...
[MESSAGE &name& &age& &region& being printed]
[PAUSE]
[OTHERWISE]
[MESSAGE &name& &age& &region& not being printed]
[PAUSE]
[END CONDITION]

Using another text file—chain printing

Option MailMerge Insert document
^OMI   { = and Alt}

Question: Document to be inserted?
Answer: Type the filename. For example 'sales.doc'.
The drive and directory can be added if necessary.
Result displayed while editing:
[INSERT DOCUMENT sales.doc]
Result when printing: the complete document inserted is printed. WordStar 2000 remembers what document it had been printing before, and prints the rest of it after the inserted document.

Insert can be used an unlimited number of times to chain complete documents. It can be used up to four times for nesting files within each other.

Windows

Up to three files can be displayed on the screen at the same time. The screen is divided horizontally into windows, with one file displayed in each. There is a ruler line at the top of each one. The cursor is visible and active in one only. It can be moved to another by the ^CW command, Cursor to Window. The status line at the top of the screen gives information for the document containing the cursor.

Before opening a window it is advisable to increase the space available by hiding the editing menu. Type ^GGS for Get Sub-menus. When experienced in using WordStar 2000 you may prefer ^GGN for Get No menus. You can always have the menu displayed again by typing ^GGA for Get All menus.

The first document is chosen for editing by selecting E from the opening menu. Another document can now be opened for viewing or editing by typing ^OW, Open a Window. The window for the new document appears at the bottom of the screen.

Open a Window
^OW {F3} This command is on the Options menu. The Choose a Name screen is displayed (see page 29).

Question: Document to edit or create?
Answer: Move highlighting or type file name, with path if necessary.

If opening a document for the first time, you will be asked to choose a format.

The cursor will be in the window which has just been opened. To move it to another window use ^CW.

Move Cursor to a Window
^CW {F3 and Shift} This moves the cursor to the next window down. If the cursor is in the bottom window, it moves it to the top window. The cursor moves to the last position it had in that window.

Once the cursor is in a window, all editing operations can be carried out. ^QP for Quit and Print cannot be used if windows are open.

Part of the top window may be hidden by a sub-menu or name display while a command is executed. Use of ^V from a Choose a Name screen, or ^GGN from menus, reduces the amount of information displayed.

There can be more than one window open on the same document. One of them has to be closed by ˆQA, Quit and Abandon, before the other can be closed by ˆQS, Quit and Save. Make sure you only make changes in one of them. WordStar 2000 allows you to make changes in both, but does not allow you to save both. If you have text in both that you want to save, use block moves to transfer all changed portions of text into one window.

If you want the other window to show changes you have made to the file in this session, use ˆQC, Quit and Continue, before you open the second window.

Moving text from one window to another

Text can be moved from one window to the other by block operations, or by 'Remove' and 'Undo'.

To copy a block from one window to another, first mark it in the window from which it is to be copied using ˆBB, Block Beginning, and ˆBE, Block End. Move the cursor to the other window, then to the place in that window where the block is required. Type ˆBC, Block Copy. The marked block will be inserted at the cursor position.

'Undo' takes the last text removed from any window and inserts it at the current cursor position. This applies for all the commands that can remove more than a single character.

If, for example, you want to copy a paragraph from one window to another, move the cursor into the paragraph to be copied. Type ^RP, Remove Paragraph, then ^U, Undo. The text in this window is now the same as before the remove command, but the paragraph has been stored in the Undo buffer. Move the cursor to the other window by ^CW, and then to the place in the second document where the copied paragraph is required. Type ^U again. The paragraph appears at the cursor position.

There can only be a marked block in one window. A block remains marked until a ^BB or ^BE is used elsewhere.

A particular number place marker, e.g. ⟨7⟩, can only exist in one window, but there can be place markers of different numbers in different windows.

A file should be saved before it is used from another window. For example if a key glossary is edited, save it before using it again.

What can be displayed?

The file in a window need not be a WordStar 2000 document. It can be an ASCII file, a WordStar file, a data file, a key glossary, a personal dictionary, or many files generated by other programs. If you want to move text from a WordStar document to a WordStar 2000 document, use W from the opening menu to convert it first.

If you want to move part of a spreadsheet into a WordStar 2000 document, use the 'print to disk' facility of your spreadsheet program. Then open the resulting file from WordStar 2000. Take note of the extension and filename of the file. Some spreadsheets add special extensions to such files.

Closing windows

Use ^QS or ^QA to close a window. If you have just been viewing the file, or copying text from it into another window, use ^QA. If you want to save changes, use ^QS. ^QC, Quit and Continue, saves changes, leaving the window open and the cursor in it.

Manuals

The WordStar 2000 package includes 4 manuals. 'Getting Started' and 'Installation Guide' are thin booklets, 'Training Guide' and 'Reference Guide' are over 200 pages each. The optional Advanced Features of StarIndex, MailList and TelMerge are described in another manual.

The file named README on the conversion disk contains amendments and clarifications to manuals, and other useful information including a current list of printers supported.

The Installation Guide and the README file contain information about the specific computer and operating system which is useful in everyday operation as well as at installation time.

Installation

When running WordStar 2000, you use copies of the files on the original disks. Do not try to make backup copies of the WordStar 2000 disks before you read the instructions in the 'Getting Started' manual. Disks 1 and 2 are copy protected; back up copies are made by the WordStar 2000 program, not by operating system utilities.

What you need—two floppy disk system
A copy of your operating system diskette; 256 kilobytes of free memory in your computer; eight blank diskettes, or nine if you have WordStar 2000+ which includes the Advanced Features of StarIndex, MailList, and TelMerge.

One of these 8 (or 9) disks becomes a work disk which you can use for your own files. Another is a key disk, needed when starting the system. The remainder will become copies of the 6 (or 7) disks in the original package.

What you need—hard disk system
Operating system on diskette or hard disk; 256 kilobytes of free memory; 1950 kilobytes of free disk space.

What you need to know before installation
If your monitor is colour or monochrome; whether you have a graphics card; what model of printer you will be using.

Note that the README file on the conversion disk says which features of the printers are supported.

Installation process

The WordStar 2000 package contains six floppy disks (seven with the optional advanced features of WordStar 2000+). It is not possible to install WordStar 2000 just by copying those diskettes, for two reasons:

* WordStar 2000 is copy protected. Copies of the word processing program itself may only be made by the first installation program.
* WordStar 2000 has to be tailored to suit the particular computer and printer in use. The second installation program performs this tailoring, and allows some choices of options to be selected by the user.

The copy protection allows three copies to be installed. It also allows any copy to be 'uninstalled' and later installed again, for example on a hard disk instead of a floppy disk.

The installation procedures can therefore be used for any of the following:

* Install a copy of WordStar 2000 for the first time. This includes copying all six (or seven) disks and tailoring to suit the computer and printer.
* Re-install to change the tailored configuration.
* 'Uninstall' to delete the word processing program and add one back into the copy counter.
* Re-install after 'uninstall': this is the same as the original installation process, except that files other than the word processing program may not have to be copied again.

The installation procedures are described in detail in the 'Getting Started' and 'Installation Guide' manuals, with amendments and extra information in the README file on the conversion disk. The procedures will vary in detail on different computers and operating systems. The description that follows is an introduction, not a detailed set of instructions. To make it easier to run the installation programs and initiate associated operating system commands, they are controlled automatically by two procedures, AutoInstall phase 1 and AutoInstall phase 2.

Original installation

The disks are:

Conversion disk
Disk 1. Installation disk.
Disk 2. Program disk.
Disk 3. Dictionary disk.
Disk 4. Tutor disk A.
Disk 5. Tutor disk B.
Disk 6. Advanced Features disk (optional extra).

For a two floppy disk system, use operating system utilities to copy the conversion disk, disks 3, 4 and 5, and disk 6 if you have the Advanced Features.

Run AutoInstall phase 1. To do this with floppy disks, put the installation disk in drive A and a blank unformatted disk in drive B. Type 'ins−1 floppy'. With hard disk, put the installation disk in drive A; with C⟩ prompt, type 'a:ins−1 hard ws2000 6'. The screen displays detailed instructions.

AutoInstall phase 1 copies the installation disk and program disk. It subtracts one from the copy counter on the original installation disk. With a two floppy disk system, it generates a key disk.

Run AutoInstall phase 2. For floppy disk, with your new copy of the installation disk in drive A type 'ins—2 floppy'. For hard disk, with the installation disk in drive A type 'a:ins—2 hard ws2000 6'. The screen displays detailed instructions.

AutoInstall phase 2 copies the rest of the disks if you are using a hard disk. It also sets WordStar 2000 to suit the computer and printer in use. It changes settings in the operating system to ensure that 20 files can be open at once.

You can stop either phase by pressing Control and C together. The copy counter is not changed in phase 1 until you get a message telling you that WordStar 2000 has been successfully installed. In phase 2:

Choose monitor—colour or monochrome;
Choose graphics card—present or not;
Choose printer—from names listed in a set of menus.

After choosing these, with a two floppy disk system, you are asked to insert your operating system disk. WordStar 2000 checks that it allows at least 20 files open. If not, it helps you to change the number of files. The only effect on other programs is a small loss of available memory—about 500 bytes on PCDOS.

After this the Quit Installation menu is displayed. One option is Advanced Modifications. These are:

Sub-menu delay; default one second.
Beep on error; default, on.
Initial directory display; default, on.
   Change in any Choose Screen by ^V.
Display command tags; default, off.
   Change when editing by ^OD.
Initial mode overtype or insert; default, insert.
   Change when editing by ^OO.
Numeric representation; default, full stop for decimal point, comma as thousands marker, e.g. '1,234.56'.
Menu display; default, all menus displayed.
   Change when editing by ^GG.
Reprogram function keys: default, as shown on keyboard template.
Change colours on a colour monitor; default colours are listed in the *Installation Guide*.

Re-installation to change configuration

On hard disk: log on to the WordStar 2000 directory, type 'ws2ins' from the system prompt.
Answer the questions on screen.
On floppy disk: put your copy of the WordStar 2000 program (disk 1) in drive B, and your copy of the Installation program (disk 2) in drive A. From the system prompt A>, type 'ws2ins'. Answer the question. As during the original installation, the program will check that your operating system is set for 20 files open, and help you change it if necessary.

Uninstall procedure

Floppy disk system
Put the copy of the WordStar 2000 program to be uninstalled in drive B, and the original installation disk in drive A. From the system prompt A>, type 'install /u'.
Answer: F for media to be uninstalled;
Answer: A for product diskette drive (input);
Answer: B for target diskette drive (output).

Hard disk system
Put the original installation disk in drive A.
Change directory to the one containing the WordStar 2000 program; if WordStar 2000 has been installed in the standard way, this can be done by typing 'CD \WS2000' (for PCDOS—see manuals for other operating systems).
For the WordStar 2000 directory, type 'A:' to log on to drive A.
Type 'install / u'.
Answer: H for media to be uninstalled;
Answer: A for product diskette drive (input);
Answer: C for target diskette drive (output).

Re-install after uninstall

On floppy disk: run AutoInstall phase 1 and phase 2. You will need three blank floppy disks, and your operating system disk.
On hard disk: run AutoInstall phase 1. If installing on a different disk or directory from that in use before, run AutoInstall phase 2. If re-installing in the same directory from which you uninstalled, log on to it and type 'ws2ins'.

Index

Abbreviation 4, 40, 58–61, 99
Arithmetic 6, 40, 46, 72, 75
ASCII 74, 109, 115
AutoInstall 10, 32, 40, 87, 119–22
Backspace 13
Backup 10, 17, 24, 117
Backup file (.BAK) 21, 23, 25, 39
Block display 46, 72
Block operations 15, 46, 68, 71–6, 91, 114
Bold printing 48
Buffer 66
Centering 49
Character width 52, 86
Choose a Name screen 29
Close a document 16, 64-5
Colour display 46-7, 117, 121
Colour printing 51
Column 45, 52, 72, 86
Comma 75, 103, 121
Command tags 46, 121
Comment (unprinted) 46
Comparison 106–110
    AND, OR, NOT 99, 100, 109
Configuration 7, 46, 117
Control key 2, 12
Copy file 35
Copy protection 7, 117–8
Copy WordStar 2000 17
(CR) Carriage Return 2, 13
Cursor keys 12
Cursor markers 47, 68–9, 115
Cursor movement 14, 45, 67–9, 112
Cut and paste 15, 114
Data file 39, 41, 91, 115
Date 99
Decimal point 75, 121
Decimal tab 52–8
Decisions screen 31
Default answer 29, 31
Dictionary 20, 76, 91, 115
Directory 10, 31-4, 37
Display option 46, 52-4, 81

Document file 22, 23
Drive 10, 31, 37
Editing 14–15, 67
Editing menu 12, 43
Electronic mail 6
Emphasized printing 48
Enter text 40
Escape key 14, 19, 58
Filename 11, 29-30, 39, 99
    .BAK .DCT .DTA .FRM . KEY .SPL 39
File size 38
Flag column 45-6
Floppy disk 8, 26, 35, 76, 117-22
Font 50-1, 87
Footer 5, 46, 61-3, 81
Footnote 5, 46, 63, 68, 81
Form feeds 89-90
Format 4, 11, 20, 42, 52, 85-92
Function key 2, 12, 32, 41, 121
Hard disk 7, 26, 76, 117-22
Header 5, 46, 61-3, 81
Help 12, 20, 32
Highlighting 29, 46
Horiz, horizontal 45, 72, 75
Hyphenation 12, 47, 81, 89
Indent 46, 53-5
Indexing 6, 9
Insert 12, 44, 73, 112, 121
Installation 4, 7, 17, 46-7, 117-22
Installation Guide 34, 96, 116, 119
Italics 51
Justification 47-8, 88
Key disk 8, 10, 117
Key file 10, 20, 39, 91
Key glossary 4, 40, 58-61, 115
Labels 108
Line number 44, 99
Line spacing 50, 86, 88
Locate 80-4
Log on 10
Long form 60
Lost file or menu 20

123

MailList 6, 9, 98, 103, 116
MailMerge 23, 41, 92, 97–112
Manuals 116
Margins 6, 12, 52-6, 86-8
Menu display 11, 28, 43, 112, 121
Message while printing 102, 111
Name & address file 97, 102
Notation 2
Open a document 42
Opening menu 8-9, 27
Operating system 8, 33, 117
Options menu 61
Organized files 5, 41, 97-105
Otherwise 108
Over, Overtype 12, 44, 121
Page break 46, 89, 90
Page layout 52, 63, 85
Page number 44, 62, 67, 89, 99
Paper tray 49, 51
Path 10, 29
Print enhancements 23, 48
Print height 50, 86
Printer 23, 49-51, 66, 87, 117, 120
Printing 17-9, 23, 65, 92-6, 112
Printing problems 96
Print to disk 92, 111, 116
PRINT. SPL (file) 23, 51, 96
Program disk 9, 76
Proportional spacing 52, 86
Quit a document 16, 24, 64, 113-4
Quit WordStar 2000 38
Quote marks 103
RAM disk 17
README file 51, 96, 116, 117
Recover lost text 21
Recovery 17, 25
Reforming text 55
Remove file 36
Remove text 15, 69-71
Rename file 36

Replace 80-4
Ribbon colour 51
Ruler 12, 43, 46, 52-7, 91
Saving 64-5, 114
Screen display 5, 43
Search 80-4
Security copy 7, 17, 24-5
Short form 61
Sorting 6, 46, 72, 74
Space 22, 38
Spelling 4, 40, 76-9
Spreadsheet 41, 116
Standard text 12, 42, 85, 90
StarIndex 6, 9, 116
Starting 26, 42
Status line 12, 43, 44, 112
Stopping 18, 19, 38, 95
Strikeout 48
Subscript, superscript 48
Tab key 12, 57
Tabs 6, 46, 52-8, 88, 91
Tags 46, 87, 84
TelMerge 6, 9, 116
Time 99
Training aids 39
Typeface 50-1
Typewriter mode 65
Typing 11, 40, 43
Underline 48, 89, 90
Undo 6, 15, 21, 70, 114
Unformatted file 44, 91
Uninstall 7, 17, 118, 122
Variables 98-106
Vert, Vertical 45, 72, 74-5
Wild card 80, 84
Windows 6, 22, 41, 44-5, 68, 72, 111-7
WordStar 9
Word-wrap 47, 66
Work disk 8, 117
Write block to file 74, 91
WS2000 (directory) 8, 11
WS2000.EXE program 17, 25

124